MAYDAYS, MAYPOLES, AND MORRIS DANCING

BY

JOHN BRAND

MAY-DAY CUSTOMS.

—— " If thou lov'st me then,
Steal forth thy father's house to-morrow night;
And in the wood, a league without the town,
Where I did met thee once with Helena,
To do observance for a morn of May,
There will I stay for thee."
Mids. Night's Dream, Act i. sc. 1.

IT was anciently the custom for all ranks of people to go out a Maying early on the first of May. Bourne tells us that in his time, in the villages in the North of England, the juvenile part of both sexes were wont to rise a little after midnight on the morning of that day, and walk to some neighbouring wood, accompanied with music and the blowing of horns, where they broke down branches from the trees and adorned them with nosegays and crowns of flowers. This done, they returned homewards with their booty about the time of sunrise, and made their doors and windows triumph in the flowery spoil.

Stubbs, in the Anatomie of Abuses, 1585, f. 94, says:—"Against Maie, every parishe, towne, and village, assemble themselves together, bothe men, women, and children, olde and yong, even all indifferently: and either goyng all together, or devidyng themselves into companies, they goe some to the woodes and groves, some to the hilles and mountaines, some to one place, some to another, where they spende all the night in pastymes, and in the mornyng they returne, bringing with them birch, bowes, and braunches of trees to deck their assemblies withall. I have heard it credibly reported (and that *viva voce*) by men of great gravitie, credite, and reputation, that of fourtie, threescore, or a hundred maides goyng to the woode over night, there have scarcely the thirde parte of them returned home againe undefiled."

Hearne, in his Preface to Robert of Gloucester's Chronicle, p. 18, speaking of the old custom of drinking out of horns, observes:—"'Tis no wonder, therefore, that upon *the jollities on the first of May* formerly, the custom of *blowing with*, and drinking in, *horns* so much prevailed, which, though it be now generally disus'd, yet the custom of blowing them *prevails at this season, even to this day, at Oxford*, to remind people of the pleasantness of that part of the year, which ought to create mirth and gayety, such as is sketch'd out in some old Books of Offices, such as the Prymer of Salisbury, printed at Rouen, 1551, 8vo." Aubrey, in his Remains of Gentilisme and Juadisme, MS. Lansd. 266, f. 5, says:—"Memorandum, at Oxford, the boys do blow *cows' horns* and *hollow canes* all night; and on May Day the young maids of every parish carry about garlands of flowers, which afterwards they hang up in their churches." Mr. Henry Rowe, in a note in his Poems, ii. 4, says:—"The Tower of Magdalen College, Oxford, erected by Cardinal Wolsey, when bursar of the College, 1492, contains a musical peal of ten bells, and *on May Day the choristers assemble on the top to usher in the spring.*" Dr. Chandler, however, in his Life of Bishop Waynflete, assures us that Wolsey had no share in the erection of the structure; and Mr. Chalmers, in his History of the University, refers the origin of the custom to a mass or requiem, which, before the Reformation, used to be annually performed on the top of the tower, for the soul of Henry VII. "This was afterwards commuted," he observes, "for a few pieces of musick, which are executed by the choristers, and for which the Rectory of Slimbridge, in Gloucestershire, pays annually the sum of 10*l*."

In Herrick's Hesperides, p. 74, are the following allusions to customs on May Day :—

> "Come, my Corinna, come: and comming, marke
> How each field turns a street, each street a park
> Made green and trimmed with trees: see how
> Devotion gives each house a bough,
> Or branch: each porch, each doore, ere this,
> An arke, a tabernacle is,
> Made up of white-thorne neatly enterwove.
> A deale of youth, ere this, is come
> Back, and with white-thorne laden home.
> Some have dispatch'd their cakes and creame,
> Before that we have left to dreame."

[In an old ballad called the Milk-maid's Life, printed about 1630, we are told :—

> "Upon the first of May,
> With garlands fresh and gay,
> With mirth and musick sweet,
> For such a season meet,
> They passe their time away :
> They dance away sorrow,
> And all the day thorow
> Their legs doe never fayle.
> They nimbly their feet doe ply,
> And bravely try the victory
> In honour o' th' milking paile."]

There was a time when this custom was observed by noble and royal personages, as well as the vulgar. Thus we read in Chaucer's Court of Love, that, early on May Day, "fourth goth al the Court, both most and lest, to fetche the flouris fresh, and braunch, and blome." It is on record that King Henry the Eighth and Queen Katherine partook of this diversion ; and historians also mention that he with his courtiers, in the beginning of his reign, rose on May Day very early to fetch May, or green boughs, and they went with their bows and arrows, shooting to the wood. Shakespeare says (Hen. VIII.) it was impossible to make the people sleep on May morning; and (Mids. N. Dream) that they rose early to observe the right of May. The court of King James the First, and the populace, long preserved the observance of the day, as Spelman's Glossary remarks under the word Maiuma. Milton has the following beautiful song on May morning :—

> " Now the bright morning star, day's harbinger,
> Comes dancing from the East, and leads with her
> The flow'ry May, who from her green lap throws
> The yellow cowslip and the pale primrose.
>   Hail, bounteous May! that dost inspire
>   Mirth and youth, and fond desire;
>   Woods and groves are of thy dressing,
>   Hill and dale doth boast thy blessing.
> Thus we salute thee with *our early song*,
> And welcome thee, and wish thee long."

Stow, in his Survay of London, 1603, pp. 98-9, quotes from Hall an account of Henry the VIII.'s riding a Maying from Greenwich to the high ground of Shooter's-hill, with Queen Katherine his wife, accompanied with many lords and ladies. He tells us also, that " on May Day in the morning, every man, except impediment, would walke into the sweete meadowes and greene woods, there to rejoyce their spirites with the beauty and savour of sweete flowers, and with the harmony of birds praysing God in their kind. I find also, that in the moneth of May, the citizens of London, of all estates, lightly in every parish, or sometimes two or three parishes joyning togither, had their severall Mayings, and did fetch in May-poles, with diverse warlike shewes, with good archers, morice-dauncers, and other devices, for pastime all the day long, and towards the evening they had stage-playes, and bonefiers in the streetes. Of these Mayings we reade, in the raigne of Henry the Sixt, that the aldermen and shiriffes of London being, on May Day, at the Bishop of London's wood, in the parish of Stebunheath, and having there a worshipfull dinner for themselves and other commers, Lydgate the poet, that was a monke of Bery, sent to them by a pursivant a joyfull commendation of that season, containing sixteen staves in meter royall, beginning thus :—

> " Mightie Flora, goddesse of fresh flowers,
>   Which clothed hath the soyle in lustie greene,
> Made buds spring with her sweete showers,
>   By influence of the sunne-shine;
> To doe pleasance of intent full cleane,
>   Unto the States which now sit here,
> Hath Vere downe sent her owne daughter deare."

Polydore Vergil says, that " at the Calendes of Maie," not only houses and gates were garnished with boughs and flowers, but "in some places the churches, whiche fashion is derived of the Romaynes, that use the same to honour their goddesse Flora with suche ceremonies, whom they name Goddesse of Fruites." (Langley's Polyd. Verg. f. 102.)   In an account of Parish Expenses in Coates's Hist. of Reading, p. 216, 1504, we have: "It. Payed for felling and bryngyng home of the bow set in the Mercat-place, for settyng up of the same, mete and drink, viij^d."

In Vox Graculi, 1623, p. 62, under May, are the following observations :—

> " To Islington and Hogsdon runnes the streame
>   Of giddie people, to eate cakes and creame."

" May is the merry moneth: on the first day, betimes in the morning, shall young fellowes and mayds be so enveloped with a mist of wandering out of their wayes, that they shall fall into ditches, one upon another. In the afternoone, if the skie cleare up, shall be a stinking stirre at Pickehatch, with the solemne revels of morice-dancing, and the hobbie-horse so neatly presented, as if one of the masters of the parish had playd it himselfe. Against this high-day, likewise, shall be such preparations for merry meetings, that divers durty sluts shall bestow more in stuffe, lace, and making up of a gowne and a peticote, then their two yeares wages come to, besides the benefits of candles' ends and kitchen stuffe."   In Whimzies, or a True Cast of Characters, 1631, p. 132, speaking of a ruffian, the author says: "His soveraignty is showne highest at *May-games*, Wakes, Summerings, and Rushbearings."

In the old Calendar of the Romish Church so often referred

to, I find the following observation on the 30th of April: " The boys go out and seek May trees." This receives illustration from an order in a MS. in the British Museum, entitled " The State of Eton School," 1560, wherein it is stated, that on the day of St. Philip and St. James, if it be fair weather, and the master grants leave, those boys who choose it may rise at four o'clock, to gather May branches, if they can do it without wetting their feet : and that on that day they adorn the windows of the bedchamber with green leaves, and the houses are perfumed with fragrant herbs.

Misson, in his Travels in England, translated by Ozell, p. 307, says : " On the 1st of May, and the five and six days following, all the pretty young country girls that serve the town with milk dress themselves up very neatly, and borrow abundance of silver plate, whereof they make a pyramid, which they adorn with ribbands and flowers, and carry upon their heads, instead of their common milk-pails. In this equipage, accompany'd by some of their fellow milk-maids, and a bagpipe or fiddle, they go from door to door, dancing before the houses of their customers, in the midst of boys and girls that follow them in troops, and everybody gives them something." In the Dedication to Colonel Martin's Familiar Epistles, 1685, we have the following allusion to this custom : " What's a May-day milking-pail without a garland and fiddle ?" " The Mayings," says Strutt, ii. 99, " are in some sort yet kept up by the milk-maids at London, who go about the streets with their garlands, music, and dancing : but this tracing is a very imperfect shadow of the original sports ; for May-poles were set up in streets, with various martial shows, morris-dancing, and other devices, with which, and revelling and good cheer, the day was passed away. At night they rejoiced, and lighted up their bonfires."

Scott, in his Discovery of Witchcraft, p. 152, tells us of an old superstition : " To be delivered from witches, they hang in their entries (among other things) hay-thorn, otherwise white-thorn, gathered on May-day." The following divination on May-day is preserved in Gay's Shepherd's Week, 4th Pastoral :

> " Last May-day fair, I search'd to find a snail,
> That might my secret lover's name reveal:

Upon a gooseberry-bush a snail I found,
For always snails near sweetest fruit abound.
I seized the vermine ; home I quickly sped,
And on the hearth the milk-white embers spread :
Slow crawl'd the snail, and, if I right can spell,
In the soft ashes marked a curious L : .
Oh, may this wondrous omen lucky prove !
For L is found in Lubberkin and Love."

The May customs are not yet forgotten in London and its
vicinity. In the Morning Post, May 2d, 1791, it was mentioned, "that yesterday being the 1st of May, according to
annual and superstitious custom, a number of persons went
into the fields and bathed their faces with the dew on the
grass, under the idea that it would render them beautiful."

" Vain hope ! No more in choral bands unite
    Her virgin votaries, and at early dawn,
Sacred to May and Love's mysterious rites,
    Brush the light dew-drops from the spangled lawn."

I remember, too, that in walking that same morning, between Hounslow and Brentford, I was met by two distinct
parties of girls, with garlands of flowers, who begged money of
me, saying, " Pray, sir, remember the garland." The young
chimney-sweepers, some of whom are fantastically dressed in
girls' clothes, with a great profusion of brick-dust, by way of
paint, gilt paper, &c., making a noise with their shovels and
brushes, are now the most striking objects in the celebration
of May-day in the streets of London.

[May-dew was held of singular virtue in former times. Pepys,
on a certain day in May, makes this entry in his diary: "My
wife away down with Jane and W. Hewer to Woolwich, in order
to a little ayre, and to lie there to-night, and so to gather May-
dew to-morrow morning, which Mrs. Turner hath taught her is
the only thing in the world to wash her face with ; and," Pepys
adds, " I am contented with it." His reasons for contentment
seem to appear in the same line ; for he says, " I went by water
to Fox-hall, and there walked in Spring-garden." And there he
notices "a great deal of company, and the weather and garden
pleasant ; and it is very pleasant and cheap going thither, for
a man may go to spend what he will, or nothing—all as one.
But to hear the nightingale and other birds, and here a fiddler,
and there a harp, and here a jew's trump, and here laughing,

and there fine people walking, is mighty diverting," says Mr. Pepys, while his wife is gone to lie at Woolwich, " in order to a little ayre and to gather May-dew."]

I have more than once been disturbed early on May morning, at Newcastle-upon-Tyne, by the noise of a song which a woman sung about the streets, who had several garlands in her hands, and which, if I mistook not, she sold to any that were superstitious enough to buy them. It is homely and low, but it must be remembered· that our treatise is not on the sublime :—

> " Rise up, maidens ! fy for shame !
> For I've been four lang miles from hame :
> I've been gathering my garlands gay :
> Rise up, fair maids, and take in your May."[1]

[At Islip, co. Oxon, the children with their May garlands sing,—

> " Good morning, Missus and Master,
> I wish you a happy day ;
> Please to smell my garland,
> Because it is the First of May."]

The following shows a custom of *making fools* on the 1st of May, like that on the 1st of April : " U. P. K. spells May Goslings," is an expression used by boys at play, as an insult to the losing party. U.P.K. is " up pick," that is, up with your pin or peg, the mark of the goal. An additional punishment was thus : the winner made a hole in the ground with his heel, into which a peg about three inches long was driven, its top being below the surface ; the loser, with his hands tied behind him, was to pull it up with his teeth, the boys buffeting with their hats, and calling out, " Up pick, you May Gosling," or " U.P.K. Gosling in May." A May Gosling on the 1st of May is made with as much eagerness in the north of England,

---

[1] Here is no pleonasm. It is simply, as the French have it, your *May.* In a Royal Household Account, communicated by Craven Ord, Esq., I find the following article : " July 7, 7 Hen. VII. Item, to the maydens of Lambeth for a May, 10*sh*." So among the Receipts and Disbursements of the Canons of the Priory of St. Mary, in Huntingdon, in Nichols's Illustrations of the Manners and Expenses of Ancient Times in England, 1797, p. 294, we have : " Item, gyven to the Wyves of Herford to the makyng of there May, 12*d*."

as an April Noddy (Noodle), or Fool, on the 1st of April."—
Gent. Mag. for April, 1791, p. 327.

[If, however, a May gosling was made on the second of the
month, the following rhyme was uttered to turn the ridicule :

> " May-day's past and gone;
> Thou's a gosling, and I'm none."]

To May-Day sports may be referred the singular bequest
of Sir Dudley Diggs (mentioned in Hasted's Kent, ii. 787),
who, by his last will, dated in 1638, left the yearly sum of
20*l*., "to be paid to two young men and two maids, who, on
May 19th, yearly, should *run a tye* at *Old Wives Lees in
Chilham*, and prevail; the money to be paid out of the profits
of the land of this part of the manor of Selgrave, which
escheated to him after the death of Lady Clive. These lands,
being in three pieces, lie in the parishes of Preston and
Faversham, and contain about forty acres, all commonly called
the *Running Lands*. Two young men and two young maids
run at *Old Wives Lees* in Chilham, yearly, on May 1st, and
the same number at Sheldwich Lees on the Monday following,
by way of trial: and the two which prevail at each of those
places run for the 10*l*. at Old Wives Lees, as above mentioned,
on May 19th." A great concourse of the neighbouring gentry
and inhabitants constantly assemble there on this occasion.
"There was, till of late years," says the same writer (Hist.
of Kent, ii. 284), " a singular, though a very ancient, custom
kept up, of electing a Deputy to the Dumb Borsholder of
Chart, as it was called, claiming liberty over fifteen houses in
the precinct of Pizein-well; every householder of which was
formerly obliged to pay the keeper of this Borsholder one
penny yearly. This Dumb Borsholder was always first called
at the Court-Leet holden for the hundred of Twyford, when
its keeper, who was yearly appointed by that court, held it
up to his call, with a neckcloth or handkerchief put through
the iron ring fixed at the top, and answered for it. This
Borsholder of Chart, and the Court-Leet, has been discontinued
about fifty years : and the Borsholder, who is put in by the
Quarter Sessions for Watringbury, claims over the whole
parish. This Dumb Borsholder is made of wood, about three
feet and half an inch long, with an iron ring at the top, and
four more by the sides, near the bottom, where it has a square

iron spike fixed, four inches and a half long, to fix it in the ground, or, on occasion, to break open doors, &c., which used to be done, without a warrant of any justice, on suspicion of goods having been unlawfully come by and concealed in any of these fifteen houses. It is not easy at this distance of time, to ascertain the origin of this dumb officer. Perhaps it might have been made use of as a badge or ensign by the office of the market here. The last person who acted as deputy to it was one Thomas Clampard, a blacksmith, whose heirs have it now in their possession."

In the Laws of the Market, printed by Andrew Clark, printer to the Honourable City of London, 1677, under "The Statutes of the Streets of this City against Noysances," 29, I find the following: "No man shall go in the streets by night or by day with bow bent, or arrows under his girdle, nor with sword unscabbar'd, under pain of imprisonment; or with hand-gun, having therewith powder and match, except it be in a usual *May-game* or *Sight*."

Audley, in a Companion to the Almanack, 1802, p. 21, says: "Some derive May from *Maia*, the mother of Mercury, to whom they offered sacrifices on the first day of it; and this seems to explain the custom which prevails on this day where the writer resides (Cambridge), of children having a figure dressed in a grotesque manner, called a *May Lady*, before which they set a table, having on it wine, &c. They also beg money of passengers, which is considered as an offering to the *maulkin;* for their plea to obtain it is, ' *Pray remember the poor May Lady.*' Perhaps the garlands, for which they also beg, originally adorned the head of the goddess. The bush of *hawthorn*, or, as it is called, *May*, placed at the doors on this day, may point out the first fruits of the Spring, as this is one of the earliest trees which blossoms."

Browne, in his Britannia's Pastorals, 1625, ii. 122, thus describes some of the May revellings:

> As I have seene *the Lady of the May*
> *Set in an arbour* (on a holy-day)
> *Built by the May-pole*, where the jocund swaines
> Dance with the maidens to the bagpipe's straines,
> When envious Night commands them to be gone,
> Call for the merry youngsters one by one,
> And for their well performance, soone disposes
> To this a garland interwove with roses;

> To that a carved hooke or well-wrought scrip;
> Gracing another with her cherry lip;
> To one her garter; to another then
> A hand-kerchiefe cast o'er and o'er agen:
> And none returneth emptie that hath spent
> His paines to fill their rurall meriment."

Hutchinson, in his History of Northumberland, ii. 14, tells us "that a syllabub, is prepared for the *May Feast,* which is made of warm milk from the cow, sweet cakes and wine: and a kind of divination is practised, by *fishing with a ladle for a wedding-ring,* which is dropped into it, for the purpose of prognosticating who shall be first married."

Tollet, in the description of his famous window, of which more will be said hereafter, tells us: "Better judges may decide that the institution of this festival originated from the Roman Floralia, or from the Celtic La Beltine, while I conceive it derived to us from our Gothic ancestors." Olaus Magnus de Gentibus Septentrionalibus, lib. xv. c. 8, says, "that after their long winter, from the beginning of October to the end of April, the Northern nations have a custom to welcome the returning splendour of the sun with dancing, and mutually to feast each other, rejoicing that a better season for fishing and hunting was approached." In honour of May Day the Goths and Southern Swedes had a mock battle between Summer and Winter, which ceremony is retained in the Isle of Man, where the Danes and Norwegians had been for a long time masters.

Borlase, in his curious account of the manners of Cornwall, speaking of the May Customs, says: "This usage is nothing more than a gratulation of the Spring;" and every house exhibited a proper signal of its approach, "to testify their universal joy at the revival of vegetation." He says: "An antient custom, still retained by the Cornish, is, that of decking their doors and porches on the first day of May with green boughs of sycamore and hawthorn, and of planting trees, or rather stumps of trees, before their houses."

In the Gentleman's Magazine for 1754, p. 354, a custom is alluded to, I believe, not yet entirely obsolete. The writer says, "They took places in the waggon, and quitted London early on May morning; and it being the custom in this month *for the passengers to give the waggoner at every inn a ribbon to adorn his team,* she soon discovered the origin of the proverb, ' as fine as a horse;' for, before they got to the end of their journey, the poor beasts were almost blinded by the tawdry party-coloured flowing honours of their heads."

Another writer in the Gentleman's Magazine for June, 1790, p. 520, says: "At Helstone, a genteel and populous borough-town in Cornwall, it is customary to dedicate the eighth of May to revelry (festive mirth, not loose jollity). It is called the Furry Day, supposed Flora's Day; not, I imagine, as many have thought, in remembrance of some festival instituted in honour of that goddess, but rather from the garlands commonly worn on that day. In the morning, very early, some troublesome rogues go round the streets with drums, or other noisy instruments, disturbing their sober neighbours, and singing parts of a song, the whole of which nobody now recollects, and of which I know no more than that there is mention in it of ' the grey goose quill,' and of going to the green wood to bring home ' the Summer and the May-o.' And, accordingly, hawthorn flowering branches are worn in hats. The commonalty make it a general holiday; and if they find any person at work, make him ride on a pole, carried on men's shoulders, to the river, over which he is to leap in a wide place, if he can; if he cannot, he must leap in, for leap he must, or pay money. About 9 o'clock they appear before the school, and demand holiday for the Latin boys, which is invariably granted; after which they collect money from house to house. About the middle of the day they collect together, to dance hand-in-hand round the streets, to the sound of the fiddle, playing a particular tune, which they continue to do till it is dark. This they call a ' Faddy.' In the afternoon the gentility go to some farm-house in the neighbourhood, to drink tea, syllabub, &c., and return in a morris-dance to the town, where they form a Faddy, and dance through the streets till it is dark, claiming a right of going through any person's house, in at one door, and out at the other. And here it formerly used to end, and the company of all kinds to disperse quietly to their several habitations; but latterly corruptions have in this, as in other matters, crept in by degrees. The ladies, all elegantly dressed in white muslins, are now conducted by their partners to the ball-room, where they continue their dance till supper-time; after which they all faddy it out of the house, breaking off by degrees to their respective houses. The mobility imitate their superiors, and also adjourn to the several public-houses, where they continue their dance till midnight. It is, upon the whole, a very festive, jovial, and withal so sober, and, I believe, singular custom: and any attempt to search out the original of it, inserted in one of your future Magazines, will very much please and gratify DURGAN."

[I am enabled to furnish a copy of the Furry-day song, which has escaped the memory of this writer :—

> " Robin Hood and Little John,
>   They both are gone to the fair,
> And we'll go to the merry green wood,
>   And see what they do there.
> For we were up as soon as any day
>   For to fetch the summer home,
> The summer and the May, O,
>   For the summer now is come !
> Where are those Spaniards
>   That make so great a boast ?
> They shall eat the grey goose feather,
>   And we will eat the roast.
> As for the brave St. George,
>   St. George he was a knight ;
> Of all the knights in Christendom
>   St. Georgy is the right.
> God bless Aunt Mary Moses,
>   And all her powers and might,
> And send us peace in merry England,
>   Both day and night !"]

The month of May is generally considered as an unlucky time for the celebration of marriage. This is an idea which has been transmitted to us by our Popish ancestors, and was borrowed by them from the ancients.

In Sinclair's Statistical Account of Scotland, 1794, xi. 620, the minister of Callander, in Perthshire, says, the people of district " have two customs, which are fast wearing out, not only here but all over the Highlands, and therefore ought to be taken notice of while they remain. Upon the first day of May, which is called *Baltan* or *Bàl-tein*-day, all the boys in a township or hamlet meet in the moors. They cut a table in the green sod, of a round figure, by casting a trench in the ground of such circumference as to hold the whole company. They kindle a fire, and dress a repast of eggs and milk of the consistence of a custard. They knead a cake of oatmeal, which is toasted at the embers against a stone. After the custard is eaten up, they divide the cake into so many portions, as similar as possible to one another in size and shape, as there are persons in the company. They daub one of these portions all over with charcoal until it be perfectly black. They put all the bits of the cake into a bonnet. Every one, blindfold, draws out a portion. He who holds the bonnet is entitled to the last bit. Whoever draws the black bit is the devoted person who is to be sacrificed to *Baal*, whose favour they mean to implore, in rendering the year productive of the sustenance of man and beast. There is little doubt of these inhuman sacrifices having been once offered in this country as well as in the East, although they now omit the act of sacrificing, and only compel the *devoted* person to leap three times through the flames; with which the ceremonies of this festival are closed." (The other custom, supposed to have a similar mystical allusion, will be found under ALLHALLOW EVEN.) "*Bal-tein* signifies the Fire of Baal. *Baal* or *Ball* is the only word in Gaelic for a globe. This festival was probably in honour of the sun, whose return, in his apparent annual course, they celebrated, on account of his having such a visible influence, by his genial warmth, on the productions of the earth. That the Caledonians paid a superstitious respect to the sun, as was the practice among many other nations, is evident, not only by the sacrifice at Baltein, but upon many other occasions. When a Highlander goes to bathe, or to drink waters out of a consecrated fountain, he must always approach by going round the place *from East to West on the South side*, in imitation of the apparent diurnal motion of the sun. This is called in Gaelic going round the right, or the lucky way. The opposite course is the wrong, or the unlucky way. And if a person's meat or drink were to affect the wind-pipe, or come against his breath, they instantly cry out *desheal!* which is an ejaculation, praying that it may go by the right way." In the same work, v. 84, the minister of Logierait, in Perthshire, says: "On the 1st of May, O. S., a festival called *Beltan* is annually held here. It is chiefly celebrated by the cowherds, who assemble by scores in the fields to dress

15

a dinner for themselves of boiled milk and eggs. These dishes they eat with a sort of cakes baked for the occasion, and having small lumps, in the form of nipples, raised all over the surface. The cake might, perhaps, be an offering to some deity in the days of Druidism."

Pennant's account of this rural sacrifice is more minute. He tells us in his Tour in Scotland, p. 90, that, on the 1st of May, in the Highlands of Scotland, the herdsmen of every village hold their *Bel-tein*. "They cut a square trench in the ground, leaving the turf in the middle ; on that they make a fire of wood, on which they dress a large caudle of eggs, butter, oatmeal, and milk, and bring, besides the ingredients of the caudle, plenty of beer and whisky : for each of the company must contribute something. The rites begin with spilling some of the caudle on the ground, by way of libation : on that, every one takes a cake of oatmeal, upon which are raised nine square knobs, each dedicated to some particular being, the supposed preserver of their flocks and herds, or to some particular animal, the real destroyer of them. Each person then turns his face to the fire, breaks off a knob, and, flinging it over his shoulders, says : ' *This I give to thee, preserve thou my horses ;*' ' *This to thee, preserve thou my sheep* ; and so on. After that they use the same ceremony to the noxious animals. ' *This I give to thee, O fox ! spare thou my lambs !*' ' *this to thee, O hooded crow !*' ' *this to thee, eagle !*' When the ceremony is over, they dine on the caudle ; and, after the feast is finished, what is left is hid by two persons deputed for that purpose ; but on the next Sunday they reassemble, and finish the reliques of the first entertainment."

I found the following note in p. 149 of the Muses' Threnodie, 1774 : " We read of a cave called ' The Dragon Hole,' in a steep rock on the face of Kinnoul Hill, of very difficult and dangerous access. On the first day of May, during the era of Popery, a great concourse of people assembled at that place to celebrate superstitious games, now (adds the writer) unknown to us, which the Reformers prohibited under heavy censures and severe penalties, of which we are informed from the ancient records of the Kirk Session of Perth."

Martin, in his Account of the Western Islands of Scotland (ed. 1716, p. 7), speaking of the Isle of Lewis, says, that " the natives in the village Barvas retain an ancient custom of sending a man very early to cross Barvas river, every first day of May, to prevent any females crossing it first; for that, they say, would hinder the salmon from coming into the river all the year round." They pretend to have learned this from a foreign sailor, who was shipwrecked upon that coast a long time ago. This observation they maintain to be true, from experience.

For an account of the custom called *Hobby-horsing*, on the 1st of May, at Minehead, county Somerset, see Savage's History of the Hundred of Carhampton, p. 583.

Sir Henry Piers, in his Description of Westmeath, 1682, tells us that the Irish "have a custom every May Day, which they count their first day of Summer, to have to their meal one formal dish, whatever else they have, which some call stir-about, or hasty-pudding, that is, flour and milk boiled thick; and this is holden as an argument of the good wife's good huswifery, that made her corn hold out so well as to have such a dish to begin summer fare with; for if they can hold out so long with bread, they count they can do well enough for what remains of the year till harvest; for then milk becomes plenty, and butter, new cheese, and curds, and sham-rocks, are the food of the meaner sort all this season. Nevertheless, in this mess, on this day, they are so formal, that even in the plentifullest and greatest houses, where bread is in abundance all the year long, they will not fail of this dish, nor yet they that for a month before wanted bread." Camden, in his Antient and Modern Manners of the Irish, says: "They fancy a green bough of a tree, fastened on May Day against the house, will produce plenty of milk that summer." General Vallancey, in his Essay on the Antiquity of the Irish Language, 1772, p. 19, speaking of the 1st of May, says: "On that day the Druids drove all the cattle through the fires, to preserve them from disorders the ensuing year. This Pagan custom is still observed in Munster and Connaught, where the meanest cottager, worth a cow and a wisp of straw, practises the same on the first day of May, and with the same superstitious ideas."

In the Survey of the South of Ireland, p. 233, we read something similar to what has been already quoted from the Statistical Account of Scotland. "The sun," says the writer, "was propitiated here by sacrifices of fire: one was on the

1st of May, for a blessing on the seed sown. The 1st of May is called in the Irish language *La Beal-tine,* that is, the day of Beal's fire. Vossius says it is well known that Apollo was called Belinus, and for this he quotes Herodian, and an inscription at Aquileia, *Apollini Belino.* The Gods of Tyre were Baal, Ashtaroth, and all the Host of Heaven, as we learn from the frequent rebukes given to the backsliding Jews for following after Sidonian idols: and the Phenician Baal, or Baalam, like the Irish Beal, or Bealin, denotes the sun, as Asturoth does the moon."

Aubrey, in his Remains of Gentilisme, MS. Lansd. 226, informs us that, " 'Tis commonly say'd in Germany that the witches do meet in the night before the first day of May, upon an high mountain, called the Blocksberg, situated in Ascanien where they, together with the devils, do dance and feast; and the common people doe, the night before the said day, fetch a certain thorn, and stick it at their house-door, believing the witches can then doe them no harm."

Dr. Clarke, in his Travels in Russia, 1810, i. 110, speaking of the "First of May," says : "The promenades at this season of the year (during Easter) are, amongst the many sights in Moscow, interesting to a stranger. The principal is on the 1st of May, Russia style, in a forest near the city. It affords a very interesting spectacle to strangers, because it is frequented by the bourgeoisie as well as by the nobles, and the national costume may then be observed in its greatest splendour. The procession of carriages and persons on horseback is immense. Beneath the trees, and upon the green sward, Russian peasants are seen seated in their gayest dresses, expressing their joy by shouting and tumultuous songs. The music of the Balalaika, the shrill notes of rustic pipes, clapping of hands, and the wild dances of the gipsies, all mingle in one revelry."

Bourne cites Polydore Vergil as telling us that, among the Italians, the youth of both sexes were accustomed to go into the fields on the Calends of May, and bring thence the branches of trees, singing all the way as they came, and so place them on the doors of their houses. This, he observes, is a relic of an ancient custom among the Heathens, who observed the four last days of April, and the first of May, in honour of the goddess Flora, who was imagined the deity presiding over the fruit and flowers : a festival that was observed with all manner of obscenity and lewdness. Dr. Moresin follows Polydore Vergil in regard to the origin of this custom.

[It was an old custom in Suffolk in most of the farm-houses, that any servant who could bring in a branch of haw-thorn in full blossom on the 1st of May, was entitled to a dish of cream for breakfast. This custom is now disused, not so much from the reluctance of the masters to give the reward, as from the inability of the servants to find the white-thorn in flower. To this custom the following stupid jingle ap-pears to belong,—

> " This is the day,
> And here is our May,
> The finest ever seen,
> It is fit for the queen ;
> So pray, ma'am, give us a cup of your cream."

A gentleman residing at Hitchin, in Hertfordshire, commu-nicated to Mr. Hone a curious account of the way in which May-day is observed at that place. The Mayers there express their judgment of the estimableness of the characters of their neighbours by fixing branches upon their doors before morn-ing ; those who are unpopular find themselves marked with nettle or some other vile weed instead. "Throughout the day parties of these Mayers are seen dancing and frolicking in va-rious parts of the town. The group that I saw .to day, which remained in Bancroft for more than an hour, was composed as follows :—First came two men with their faces blacked, one of them with a birch broom in his hand, and a large artificial hump on his back ; the other dressed as a woman, all in rags and tatters, with a large straw bonnet on, and carrying a ladle: these are called ' Mad Moll and her husband.' Next came two men, one most fantastically dressed with ribbons, and a great variety of gaudy-coloured silk handkerchiefs tied round his arms, from the shoulders to the wrists, and down his thighs and legs to the ankles ; he carried a drawn sword in his hand ; leaning upon his arm was a youth dressed as a fine lady, in white muslin, and profusely bedecked from top to toe with gay ribbons ; these, I understood, were called the ' Lord and Lady of the company.' After these followed six or seven couples more, attired much in the same style as the lord and lady, only the men were without swords. When this group received a satisfactory contribution at any house, the music struck up from a violin, clarionet, and fife, accompanied by the long drum, and they began the merry dance, and very well they danced, I assure you; the men-*women* looked and footed it so much like *real* women, that I stood in great doubt as to which sex they belonged to, till Mrs. J. assured me that women were not permitted to mingle in these sports. While the dancers were merrily footing it, the principal amusement to the populace was caused by the grimaces and clownish tricks of Mad Moll and her husband. When the circle of spectators became so contracted as to interrupt the dancers, then Mad Moll's husband went to work with his broom, and swept the road dust all round the circle into the faces of the crowd; and when any pretended affronts were offered (and many were offered) to his wife, he pursued the offenders, broom in hand; if he could not overtake them, whether they were males or females, he flung his broom at them. These flights and pursuits caused an abundance of merriment. The Hitchin Mayers have a song, much in the style of a Christmas Carol, which Mr. Hone has also given :—

> " Remember us, poor Mayers all,
>   And thus do we begin
> To lead our lives in righteousness,
>   Or else we die in sin.
>
> We have been rambling all this night,
>   And almost all this day;
> And now returned back again,
>   We have brought you a branch of May.
>
> A branch of May we have brought you,
>   And at your door it stands;
>   It is but a sprout,
>   But it's well budded out
> By the work of our Lord's hands.
>
> The hedges and trees they are so green,
>   As green as any leek;
> Our heavenly Father he watered them
>   With his heavenly dew so sweet.
>
> The heavenly gates are open wide,
>   Our paths are beaten plain,
> And if a man be not too far gone,
>   He may return again.

> The life of man is but a span,
> It flourishes like a flower;
> We are here to-day and gone to-morrow
> And we are dead in an hour.
>
> The moon shines bright, and the stars give a light,
> A little before it is day;
> So God bless you all, both great and small,
> And send you a joyful May!"

In London, May-day was once as much observed as it was in any rural district. There were several May-poles throughout the city, particularly one near the bottom of Catherine-street, in the Strand, which, rather oddly, became in its latter days a support for a large telescope at Wanstead in Essex, the property of the Royal Society. The milkmaids were amongst the last conspicuous celebrators of the day. They used to dress themselves in holiday guise on this morning, and come in bands with fiddles, whereto they danced, attended by a strange-looking pyramidal pile, covered with pewter plates, ribands, and streamers, either borne by a man upon his head, or by two men upon a hand-barrow: this was called their *garland*. The young chimney-sweepers also made this a peculiar festival, coming forth into the streets in fantastic dresses, and making all sorts of unearthly noises with their shovels and brushes. The benevolent Mrs. Montagu, one of the first of the class of literary ladies in England, gave these home slaves an annual dinner on this day, in order, we presume, to aid a little in reconciling them to existence. In London, May-day still remains the great festival of the sweeps, and much finery and many vagaries are exhibited on the occasion.

The following account of May-day in the streets of London in 1844, is extracted from the *Times* of the following day :—
" Yesterday being May-day, the more secluded parts of the metropolis were visited by Jack-in-the-Green, and the usual group of grotesque attendants. Among numerous displays of this nature, the only one that exhibited any novelty was a group of tinselled holiday-makers, attended, not by the usual ' My lady,' with a gilt ladle, but by a very sturdy-looking impersonation of the ' Pet of the ballet,' attired in a remarkably short gauze petticoat, beneath which were displayed a pair of legs and ankles that had certainly been brought to a most extraordinary state of muscular development. This strapping repre-

sentative of stage elegance was attended by a protector in the somewhat anomalous garb of Jem Crow, and who addressed his lady by the title of ' Marmselle Molliowski,' introducing her to the spectators as a foreign dancer of notoriety, who had that day condescended to make her first appearance in public by dancing the polka as it really ought to be danced, and in such a manner as would at once satisfy everybody that it was the most extraordinary dance ever invented. After this introduction, Marmselle Molliowski went through a most facetious burlesque, combining all the various absurdities of stage dancing, and ending, by way of climax, with a regular summerset ; and the somewhat lavish display of a pair of yellow buckskins, the discovery of which, together with a mock curtesy that terminated the performance, excited shouts of laughter among the multitude, who rewarded the very masculine-looking Mademoiselle Molliowski with a heavy shower of ' browns.' "

I am induced to give at length a very interesting communication on this anniversary by Mr. L. Jewitt, printed in the Literary Gazette, May, 1847 :—" While you are deafened by the discordant sounds of the drums and other instruments, and the host of hooting boys, accompanying Jack-in-the-Green in his perambulations through your busy streets, and while you are bewildered by the giddy whirling dance of the sooty monarch under the green extinguisher, and his gay attendants, with their flaunting ribands, their flowers, their brass ladles, and tinsel, the cocked hats and court dresses of the males, and the rustic broad-brimmed straws, the short white dresses, and graceful sylph-like movements of the chummy females, it will be a relief to you to turn and contemplate the pretty and simple celebration of this ' sweet May-day' in a quiet country village. And now the milkmaids' garlands are no more, and the dancing round the Maypole has passed away, and other May customs and ceremonies are fast being buried in that oblivion where many remnants of the habits and superstitions of our forefathers have long been laid, it will be pleasant to you to know that in some secluded spots May-day customs are still observed, and are looked forward to with as much interest as ever. In Oxford, the singing at Magdalen College still takes place, as you are aware, on the top of the magnificent tower. The choristers assemble there in their white gowns, at a little before five o'clock in the morning, and as soon as the clock has struck, commence singing their matins. The beautiful bridge and all around the college are covered with spectators ; indeed it is quite a little fair ; the inhabitants of the city, as well as of the neighbouring villages, collecting together, some on foot and some in carriages, to hear the choir, and to welcome in the happy day. Hosts of boys are there too, with tin trumpets, and stalls are fitted up for the sale of them and sweetmeats ; and as soon as the singers cease, the bells peal forth their merry sounds in joyful welcome of the new month ; and the boys, who have been impatiently await- ing for the conclusion of the matins, now blow their trumpets lustily, and, performing such a chorus as few can imagine, and none forget, start off in all directions, and scour the fields and lanes, and make the woods re-echo to their sounds, in search of flowers. The effect of the singing is sweet, solemn, and almost supernatural, and during its celebration the most pro- found stillness reigns over the assembled numbers ; all seem impressed with the angelic softness of the floating sounds, as they are gently wafted down by each breath of air. All is hushed, and calm, and quiet—even breathing is almost for- gotten, and all seem lost even to themselves, until, with the first peal of the bells, the spell is broken, and noise and con- fusion usurp the place of silence and quiet. But even this custom, beautiful as it is, is not so pleasing and simple as the one observed at Headington, two miles from Oxford, where the children carry garlands from house to house. They are all alert some days beforehand, gathering evergreens, and levy- ing contributions of flowers on all who possess gardens, to decorate their sweet May offerings. Each garland is formed of a hoop for a rim, with two half hoops attached to it, and crossed above, much in the shape of a crown ; each member is beautifully adorned with flowers, and the top surmounted by a fine crown imperial, or other showy bunch of flowers. Each garland is attended by four children, two girls dressed in all their best, with white frocks, long sashes, and plenty of ribands, and each wearing a cap, tastefully ornamented with flowers, &c., who carry the garland supported betwixt them, by a stick passed through it, between the arches. These are followed by the *lord and lady*, a boy and girl, linked together by a white handkerchief, which they hold at either end, and who are dressed as gaily as may be in ribands, sashes, rosettes, and flowers—the 'lady' wearing a smart tasty cap, and carrying a large purse. They then go from house to house, and sing this simple verse to a very primitive tune :—

> ' Gentlemen and ladies,
>   We wish you happy May;
>   We come to show you a garland,
>   Because it is May-day.'

"One of the bearers then asks, ' Please to handsel the lord and lady's purse ;' and on some money being given, the 'lord' doffs his cap, and taking one of the ' lady's' hands in his right, and passing his left arm around her waist, kisses her ; the money is then put in the purse, and they depart to repeat the same ceremony at the next house. In the village are upwards of a dozen of these garlands, with their ' lords and ladies,' which give to the place the most gay and animated appearance."

The May Garlands are thus alluded to in Fletcher's Poems, 12mo, Lond. 1656, p. 209.

> " Heark, how Amyntas in melodious loud
> Shrill raptures tunes his horn-pipe ! whiles a crowd
> Of snow-white milk-maids, crownd with garlands gay,
> Trip it to the soft measure of his lay ;
> And fields with curds and cream like green-cheese lye ;
> This now or never is the Gallaxie.
> If the facetious Gods ere taken were
> With mortal beauties and disguis'd, 'tis here.
> See how they mix societies, and tosse
> The tumbling ball into a willing losse,
> That th' twining *Ladyes* on their necks might take
> The doubled kisses which they first did stake."]

MAY-POLES.

Bourne, speaking of the 1st of May, tells us : " The after part of the day is chiefly spent in dancing round a tall pole, which is called a May Pole ; which being placed in a convenient part of the village, stands there, as it were, consecrated to the Goddess of Flowers, without the least violation offer'd to it in the whole circle of the year." Stubbs, a puritanical writer, in his Anatomie of Abuses, says : " But their cheefest jewell they

bring from thence [the woods] is their *Maie poole*, whiche they
bring home with greate veneration, as thus :—They have
twentie or fourtie yoke of oxen, every oxe havyng a sweete
nosegaie of flowers tyed on the tippe of his hornes, and these
oxen drawe home this Maie poole (this stinckyng idoll rather),
which is covered all over with flowers and hearbes, bounde
rounde aboute with stringes, from the top to the bottome, and
sometyme painted with variable colours, with twoo or three
hundred men, women, and children followyng it with greate
devotion. And thus beyng reared up, with handkerchiefes
and flagges streamyng on the toppe, they strawe the grounde
aboute, binde greene boughes about it, sett up sommer haules,
bowers, and arbours, hard by it. And then fall they to ban-
quet and feast, to leape and daunce aboute it, as the Heathen
people did at the dedication of their idolles, whereof this is a
perfect patterne, or rather the thyng itself."

[No essay on this subject can be considered complete without the curious old ballad in the *Westminster Drollery*, called
the " Rural Dance about the May-pole, the tune the first
figure dance at Mr. Young's ball, May 1671 :"—

> " Come lasses and lads, take leave of your dads,
>   And away to the May-pole hie;
> For every he has got him a she,
>   And the minstrel's standing by.
> For Willy has gotten his Jill, and Johnny has got his Joan.
> To jig it, jig it, jig it, jig it up and down.
>
> Strike up, says Wat. Agreed, says Kate,
>   And, I prithee, fidler, play ;
> Content, says Hodge, and so says Madge,
>   For this is a holiday!
> Then every man did put his hat off to his lass,
> And every girl did curchy, curchy, curchy on the grass.
>
> Begin, says Hall. Aye, aye, says Mall,
>   We'll lead up *Packington's Pound :*
> No, no, says Noll. And so, says Doll,
>   We'll first have, *Sellenger's Round.*
> Then every man began to foot it round about,
> And every girl did jet it, jet it, jet it in and out.
>
> You're out, says Dick. 'Tis a lie, says Nick ;
>   The fiddler played it false :
> 'Tis true, says Hugh ; and so says Sue,
>   And so says nimble Alce.
> The fiddler then began to play the tune again,
> And every girl did trip it, trip it, trip it to the men."

"I shall never forget," says Washington Irving, "the delight I felt on first seeing a May-pole. It was on the banks of the Dee, close by the picturesque old bridge that stretches across the river from the quaint little city of Chester. I had already been carried back into former days by the antiquities of that venerable place, the examination of which is equal to turning over the pages of a black-letter volume, or gazing on the pictures in Froissart. The May-pole on the margin of that poetic stream completed the illusion. My fancy adorned it with wreaths of flowers, and peopled the green bank with all the dancing revelry of May-day. The mere sight of this May-pole gave a glow to my feelings, and spread a charm over the country for the rest of the day; and as I traversed a part of the fair plain of Cheshire, and the beautiful borders of Wales, and looked from among swelling hills down a long green valley, through which ' the Deva wound its wizard stream,' my imagination turned all into a perfect Arcadia."]

In Vox Graculi, 1623, p. 62, speaking of May, the author says: "This day shall be erected long wooden *idols*, called May-poles; whereat many greasie churles shall murmure, that will not bestow so much as a faggot-sticke towards the warming of the poore: an humour that, while it seems to smell of *conscience*, savours indeed of nothing but *covetousness*." Stevenson, in the Twelve Moneths, 1661, p. 22, says, "The tall young oak is cut down for a May-pole, and the frolick fry of the town prevent the rising of the sun, and, with joy in their faces and boughs in their hands, they march before it to the place of erection." I find the following in A Pleasant Grove of New Fancies, 1657, p. 74:—

> "The Maypole is up,
>   Now give me the cup,
> I'll drink to the garlands around it,
>   But first unto those
>   Whose hands did compose
> The glory of flowers that crown'd it."[1]

In Northbrooke's Treatise, wherein Dicing, Dauncing, vaine Playes or Enterluds, with other idle Pastimes, &c., commonly used on the Sabbath-day, are reproved, 1577, p. 140, is the

---

[1] In the Chapel-wardens' Accounts of Brentford, 1623, is the following article: "Received for the Maypole £1 4s." Lysons's Envir. of Lond. ii. 54.

following passage : " What adoe make our yong men at the time of May ? Do they not use night-watchings to rob and steale yong trees out of other men's grounde, and bring them into their parishe, with minstrels playing before : and when they have set it up, they will decke it with floures and garlands, and daunce rounde (men and women togither, moste unseemely and intolerable, as I have proved before) about the tree, like unto the children of Israell that daunced about the golden calfe that they had set up."

Owen, in his Welsh Dictionary, in v. *Bedwen*, a birch-tree, explains it also by " a May-pole, because it is always (he says) made of birch. It was customary to have games of various sorts round the bedwen ; but the chief aim, and on which the fame of the village depended, was to preserve it from being stolen away, as parties from other places were continually on the watch for an opportunity, who, if successful, had their feats recorded in songs on the occasion."

Tollett, in the account of his painted window, printed in the Variorum Shakespeare, tells us, that the May-pole there represented " is painted yellow and black, in spiral lines." Spelman's Glossary mentions the custom of erecting a tall May-pole, painted with various colours : and Shakespeare, in A Midsummer Night's Dream, iii. 2, speaks of a painted May-pole. " Upon our pole," adds Tollett, " are displayed St. George's red cross, or the banner of England, and a white penon or streamer, emblazoned with a red cross, terminating like the blade of a sword, but the delineation thereof is much faded."[1] Keysler, in p. 78 of his Northern and Celtic Antiquities, gives us, perhaps, the origin of May-poles ;' and that the French used to erect them appears also from Mezeray's History of their King Henry IV., and from a passage in Stow's Chronicle in the year 1560. Mr. Theobald and Dr. Warburton acquaint us that the May-games, and particularly some

---

[1] Lodge, in his Wit's Miserie, 1596, p. 27, describing Usury, says : " His spectacles hang beating *like the flag in the top of a May-pole.*" Borlase, speaking of the manners of the Cornish people, says, " From towns they make incursions, on May Eve, into the country, cut down a tall elm, bring it into the town with rejoicings, and having fitted a straight taper pole to the end of it, and painted it, erect it in the most public part, and upon holidays and festivals dress it with garlands of flowers, or *ensigns and streamers.*"

of the characters in them, became exceptionable to the puritanical humour of former times. By an ordinance of the [Long] Parliament, in April, 1644, all May-poles were taken down, and removed by the constables, churchwardens, &c. After the Restoration they were permitted to be erected again.

By Charles I.'s warrant, dated Oct. 18, 1633, it was enacted, that, " for his good people's lawfull recreation, after the end of Divine Service, his good people be not disturbed, letted, or discouraged from any lawfull recreation; such as dancing, either men or women; archery for men, leaping, vaulting, or any other such harmless recreations : nor from having of May Games, Whitson Ales, and Morris Dances, and *the setting up of May-poles*, and other sports therewith used; so as the same be had in due and convenient time, without impediment or neglect of Divine Service. And that women shall have leave to carry rushes to the church for the decorating of it, according to their old custom. But withal his Majesty doth hereby account still as prohibited, all unlawful games to be used on Sundays only, as bear and bull-baitings, interludes, and, at all times, in the meaner sort of people by law prohibited, bowling." (Harris's Life of Charles I., p. 48.) The following were the words of the ordinance for their destruction, 1644 : " And because the prophanation of the Lord's Day hath been heretofore greatly occasioned by May-poles, (a heathenish vanity, generally abused to superstition and wickednesse,) the Lords and Commons do further order and ordain that all and singular May-poles, that are or shall be erected, shall be taken down and removed by the constables, borsholders, tything-men, petty constables, and churchwardens of the parishes, when the same shall be; and that no May-pole shall be hereafter set up, erected, or suffered to be within this kingdom of England, or dominion of Wales. The said officers to be fined five shillings weekly till the said May-pole be taken downe."

In Burton's Judgments upon Sabbath Breakers, a work written professedly against the Book of Sports, 1641, are some curious particulars illustrating May-games, p. 9, Example 16:—"At Dartmouth, 1634, upon the coming forth and publishing of the Book of Sports, a company of yonkers, on May-day morning, before day, went into the country to fetch home a May-pole with drumme and trumpet, whereat the neighbouring inhabitants were affrighted, supposing some enemies had landed to sack them. The pole being thus brought home, and set up, they began to drink healths about it, and to it, till they could not stand so steady as the pole did : whereupon the mayor and justice bound the ringleaders over to the sessions ; whereupon these complaining to the Archbishop's Vicar-generall, then in his visitation, he prohibited the justices to proceed against them in regard of the King's Book. But the justices acquainted him they did it for their disorder in transgressing the bounds of the book. Hereupon these libertines, scorning at authority, one of them fell suddenly into a consumption, whereof he shortly after died. Now although this revelling was not on the Lord's Day, yet being upon any other day, and especially May-day, the May-pole set up thereon giving occasion to the prophanation of the Lord's Day the whole year after, it was sufficient to provoke God to send plagues and judgments among them." The greater part of the examples are levelled at summer-poles.

In Pasquil's Palinodia, a Poem, 1634, is preserved a curious description of May-poles :

" Fairely we marched on, till our approach
    Within the spacious passage of the Strand,
Objected to our sight a summer-broach,
    Ycleap'd a May-pole, which, in all our land,
No city, towne, nor streete, can parralell,
Nor can the lofty spire of Clarken-well,
Although we have the advantage of a rocke,
Pearch up more high his turning weathercock.

Stay, quoth my Muse, and here behold a signe
    Of harmlesse mirth and honest neighbourhood,
Where all the parish did in one combine
    To mount the rod of peace, and none withstood :
When no capritious constables disturb them,
Nor justice of the peace did seeke to curb them,
Nor peevish puritan, in rayling sort,
Nor over-wise church-warden, spoyl'd the sport.

Happy the age, and harmlesse were the dayes,
    (For then true love and amity was found)
When every village did a May-pole raise,
    And Whitson-ales and May-games did abound :

And all the lusty yonkers, in a rout,
With merry lasses daunc'd the rod about,
Then Friendship to their banquets bid the guests,
And poore men far'd the better for their feasts.

The lords of castles, mannors, townes, and towers,
   Rejoic'd when they beheld the farmers flourish,
And would come downe unto the summer bowers
   To see the country gallants dance the morrice.

But since the summer poles were overthrown,
   And all good sports and merriment decay'd,
How times and men are changed, so well is knowne,
   It were but labour lost if more were said.

Alas, poore May-poles ! what should be the cause
   That you were almost banish't from the earth ?
Who never were rebellious to the lawes;
   Your greatest crime was harmlesse honest mirth :
What fell malignant spirit was there found,
To cast your tall pyramides to ground ?
To be some envious nature it appeares,
That men might fall together by the eares.

Some fiery, zealous brother, full of spleene,
   That all the world in his deepe wisdom scornes,
Could not endure the May-pole should be seene
   To weare a coxe-combe higher than his hornes :
He took it for an idoll, and the feast
For sacrifice unto that painted beast;
Or for the wooden Trojan asse of sinne,
By which the wicked merry Greeks came in.

But I doe hope once more the day will come,
   That you shall mount and pearch your cocks as high
As e'er you did, and that the pipe and drum ,
   Shall bid defiance to your enemy ;
And that all fidlers, which in corners lurke,
And have been almost starved for want of worke,
Shall draw their crowds, and at your exaltation,
Play many a fit of merry recreation.

And you, my native town (Leeds), which was of old,
   Whenas thy bon-fires burn'd and May-poles stood,
And when thy wassall-cups were uncontrol'd
   The summer bower of peace and neighbourhood;
Although since these went down, thou lyst forlorn,
By factious schismes and humours overborne, _
Some able hand I hope thy rod will raise,
That thou mayst see once more thy happy daies.''

Douce observes that, "during the reign of Elizabeth, the Puritans made considerable havoc among the May-games by their preachings and invectives. Poor Maid Marian was assimilated to the whore of Babylon; Friar Tuck was deemed a remnant of Popery; and the Hobby-horse as an impious and Pagan superstition: and they were at length most completely put to the rout, as the bitterest enemies of religion. King James's Book of Sports restored the Lady and the Hobby-horse: but during the Commonwealth, they were again attacked by a new set of fanatics; and, together with the whole of the May festivities, the Whitsun-ales, &c., in many parts of England, degraded." (Illustr. of Shakespeare, ii. 463.) In a curious tract, entitled the Lord's loud Call to England, published by H. Jessey, 1660, there is given part of a letter from one of the Puritan party in the North, dated Newcastle, 7th of May, 1660: "Sir, the countrey, as well as the town, abounds with vanities; now the reins of liberty and licentiousness are let loose: *May-poles*, and playes, and juglers, and all things else, now pass current. Sin now appears with a brazen face," &c.[1]

In Rich's Honestie of this Age, 1615, p. 5, is the following passage: "The country swaine, that will sweare more on Sundaies, *dancing about a May-pole*, then he will doe all the week after at his worke, will have a cast at me."

In Small Poems of divers Sorts, written by Sir Aston Cokain, 1658, p. 209, is the following, *of Wakes and May-poles* :—

> "The zealots here are grown so ignorant,
> That they mistake wakes for some ancient saint,
> They else would keep that feast; for though they all
> Would be cal'd saints here, none in heaven they call:
> Besides they *May-poles* hate with all their soul,
> I think, because a Cardinal was a *Pole*."

[1] Dr. Stukeley, in his Itinerarium Curiosum, 1724, p. 29, says: There is a May-pole hill near Horn Castle, Lincolnshire, "where probably stood an Hermes in Roman times. The boys annually keep up the festival of the *Floralia* on May Day, making a procession to this hill with May gads (as they call them) in their hands. This is a white willow wand, the bark peel'd off, ty'd round with cowslips, a thyrsus of the Bacchinals. At night they have a bonefire, and other merriment, which is really a sacrifice or religious festival."

Stevenson, in the Twelve Moneths, p. 25, has these observations at the end of May :—

> " Why should the priest against the May-pole preach ?
> Alas ! it is a thing out of his reach ;
> How he the errour of the time condoles,
> And sayes, 'tis none of the cælestial poles ;
> Whilst he (fond man !) at May-poles thus perplext,
> Forgets he makes a May-game of his text.
> But May shall tryumph at a higher rate,
> Having trees for poles, and boughs to celebrate ;
> And the green regiment, in brave array,
> Like Kent's great walking grove, shall bring in May."

After the Restoration, as has been already noticed, May-poles were permitted to be erected again. Thomas Hall, however, another of the puritanical writers, published his Funebriæ Floræ, the Downfall of May Games, so late as 1660. At the end is a copy of verses,[1] from which the subsequent selection has been made :—

> " I am Sir May-pole, that's my name ;
> Men, May, and Mirth give me the same.
>
> And thus hath Flora, May, and Mirth,
> Begun and cherished my birth,
> Till time and means so favour'd mee,
> That of a twig I waxt a tree :
> Then all the people, less and more,
> My height and tallness did adore.
>
> —— under Heaven's cope,
> There's none as I so near the Pope ;
> Whereof the Papists give to mee,
> Next papal, second dignity.
> Hath holy father much adoe
> When he is chosen ? so have I too :
> Doth he upon men's shoulders ride ?
> That honour doth to mee betide :
> There is joy at my plantation,
> As is at his coronation ;
> Men, women, children, on an heap,
> Do sing, and dance, and frisk and leap ;
> Yea, drumms and drunkards, on a rout,
> Before mee make a hideous shout ;
> Whose loud alarum and blowing cries
> Do fright the earth and pierce the skies.

[1] [A copy of these lines may be seen in MS. Harl. 1221, where they are entitled, " A May-pooles speech to a traveller."]

Hath holy Pope his holy guard,
So have I to do it watch and ward.

For, where 'tis nois'd that I am come,
My followers summoned are by drum.
I have a mighty retinue,
The scum of all the raskall crew
Of fidlers, pedlers, jayle-scap't slaves,
Of tinkers, turn-coats, tospot-knaves,
Of theeves and scape-thrifts many a one,
With bouncing Besse, and jolly Jone,
With idle boyes, and journey-men,
And vagrants that their country run :
Yea, Hobby-horse doth hither prance,
Maid-Marrian and the Morrice-dance.
My summons fetcheth, far and near,
All that can swagger, roar and swear,
All that can dance, and drab and drink,
They run to mee as to a sink.
These mee for their commander take,
And I do them my black-guard make.

I tell them 'tis a time to laugh,
To give themselves free leave to quaff,
To drink their healths upon their knee,
To mix their talk with ribaldry

Old crones, that scarce have tooth or eye,
But crooked back and lamed thigh,
Must have a frisk, and shake their heel,
As if no stitch nor ache they feel.
I bid the servant disobey,
The childe to say his parents nay.
The poorer sort, that have no coin,
I can command them to purloin.
All this, and more, I warrant good,
For 'tis to maintain neighbourhood.

The honour of the Sabbath-day
My *dancing-greens* have ta'en away
Let preachers prate till they grow wood :
Where I am they can do no good."

At page 10, he says : "The most of these May-poles are
stollen, yet they give out that the poles are given them.—
There were two May-poles set up in my parish [King's Nor-
ton] ; the one was stollen, and the other was given by a
profest papist. That which was stolen was said to bee given,
when 'twas proved to their faces that 'twas stollen, and they

were made to acknowledge their offence. This poll that was stollen was rated at five shillings: if all the poles one with another were so rated, which was stollen this May, what a considerable sum would it amount to! Fightings and bloodshed are usual at such meetings, insomuch that 'tis a common saying, that 'tis *no festival unless there bee some fightings.*" "If Moses were angry," he says in another page, "when he saw the people dance about a golden calf, well may we be angry to see people dancing the morrice about a post in honour of a whore, as you shall see anon." "Had this rudeness," he adds, "been acted only in some ignorant and obscure parts of the land, I had been silent; but when I perceived that the complaints were general from all parts of the land, and that even in Cheapside itself the rude rabble had set up this ensign of profaneness, and had put the lordmayor to the trouble of seeing it pulled down, I could not, out of my dearest respects and tender compassion to the land of my nativity, and for the prevention of the like disorders (if possible) for the future, but put pen to paper, and discover the sinful rise, and vile profaneness that attend such misrule."

So, again, in Randolph's Poems, 1646,

> "These teach that dancing is a Jezabel,
> And Barley-Break the ready way to Hell;
> The Morice idols, Whitsun-Ales, can be
> But prophane reliques of a jubilee:
> There is a zeal t' expresse how much they do
> The organs hate, have silenc'd bagpipes too;
> *And harmless May-poles all are rail'd upon,*
> *As if they were the tow'rs of Babylon."*

So in the Welsh Levite tossed in a Blanket, 1691: "I remember the blessed times, when every thing in the world that was displeasing and offensive to the brethren went under the name of horrid abominable Popish superstition. Organs and May-poles, Bishop's Courts and the Bear Garden, surplices and long hair, cathedrals and play-houses, set-forms and painted glass, fonts and Apostle spoons, church musick and bull-baiting, altar rails and rosemary on brawn, nay fiddles, Whitson ale, pig at Bartholomew Fair, plum porrige, puppet shows, carriers bells, figures in gingerbread, and at last Moses and Aaron, the Decalogue, the Creeds, and the Lord's Prayer,

A crown, a cross, an angel, and bishops head, could not be endured, so much as in á sign. Our garters, bellows, and warming pans wore godly mottos, our bandboxes were lined with wholesome instructions, and even our trunks with the Assembly-men's sayings. Ribbons were converted into Bible-strings. Nay, in our zeal we visited the gardens and apothecary's shops. *Unguentum Apostolicum, Carduus benedictus, Angelica, St. John's Wort,* and *Our Ladies Thistle,* were summoned before a class, and commanded to take new names. We unsainted the Apostles."[1]

The author of the pamphlet entitled The Way to Things by Words, and Words by Things, in his specimen of an Etymological Vocabulary, considers the May-pole in a new and curious light. We gather from him that our ancestors held an anniversary assembly on May-day; and that the column of May (whence our May-pole) was the great standard of justice in the Ey-Commons or Fields of May.[2] Here it was that the people, if they saw cause, deposed or punished their governors, their barons, and their kings. The judge's bough or wand (at this time discontinued, and only faintly represented by a trifling nosegay), and the staff or rod of authority in the civil and in the military (for it was the mace of civil power, and the truncheon of the field officers), are both derived from hence. A mayor, he says, received his name from this May, in the sense of lawful power; the crown, a mark of dignity and symbol of power, like the mace and sceptre, was also taken from the May, being representative of the garland or crown, which, when hung on the top of the May or pole, was the great signal for convening the

[1] [" He rides up and down the countrey, and every town he comes at with *a May-pole,* he wonders what the Aristotelean parson and the people mean, that they do not presently cut it down, and set up such a one as is at Gresham College, or St. James's Park; and to what purpose is it to preach to people, and go about to save them, without a telescope, and a glass for fleas. And for all this, perhaps this great undervaluer of the clergie, and admirer of his own ingenuity, can scarce tell the difference between aqua fortis and aqua vitæ, or between a pipkin and a crucible." —Eachard's Observations, 8vo. 1671, p. 167.]

[2] " At Hesket (in Cumberland) yearly on St. Barnabas's Day, by the highway side, under a thorn-tree (according to the very ancient manner of holding assemblies in the open air), is kept the court for the whole Forest of Englewood."—Nicolson and Burn's Hist. of Westmor. and Cumb. ii. 344.

people; the arches of it, which spring from the circlet, and meet together at the mound or round bell, being necessarily so formed, to suspend it to the top of the pole. The word May-pole, he observes, is a pleonasm; in French it is called singly the *Mai*. He further tells us, that this is one of the most ancient customs, which from the remotest ages has been, by repetition from year to year, perpetuated down to our days, not being at this instant totally exploded, especially in the lower classes of life. It was considered as the boundary day that divided the confines of winter and summer, allusively to which there was instituted a sportful war between two parties; the one in defence of the continuance of winter, the other for bringing in the summer. The youth were divided into troops, the one in winter livery, the other in the gay habit of the spring. The mock battle was always fought booty; the spring was sure to obtain the victory, which they celebrated by carrying triumphantly green branches with May flowers, proclaiming and singing the song of joy, of which the burthen was in these or equivalent terms: "We have brought the summer home."

Keysler, says Mr. Borlase, thinks that the custom of the May-pole took its rise from the earnest desire of the people to see their king, who, seldom appearing at other times, made his procession at this time of year to the great assembly of the States held in the open air.

Sir Henry Piers, in his Description of Westmeath, in Ireland, 1682, says: "On May Eve, every family sets up before their door a green bush, strewed over with yellow flowers, which the meadows yield plentifully. In countries where timber is plentiful they erect tall slender trees, which stand high, and they continue almost the whole year; so as a stranger would go nigh to imagine that they were all signs of ale-sellers, and that all houses were ale-houses."

"A singular custom," says Ireland, in his Views of the Medway, "used to be annually observed on May Day by the boys of Frindsbury and the neighbouring town of Stroud. They met on Rochester bridge, where a skirmish ensued between them. This combat probably derived its origin from a drubbing received by the monks of Rochester in the reign of Edward I. These monks, on occasion of a long drought, set out on a procession for Frindsbury to pray for rain; but the day proving windy, they apprehended the lights would be blown out, the banners tossed about, and their order much discomposed. They therefore requested of the Master of Stroud Hospital leave to pass through the orchard of his house, which he granted without the permission of his brethren; who, when they had heard what the Master had done, instantly hired a company of ribalds, armed with clubs and bats, who way-laid the poor monks in the orchard, and gave them a severe beating. The monks desisted from proceeding that way, but soon after found out a pious mode of revenge, by obliging the men of Frindsbury, with due humility, to come yearly on Whit Monday, with their clubs, in procession to Rochester, as a penance for their sins. Hence probably came the by-word of Frindsbury Clubs."

In the British Apollo, 1708, vol. i. No. 25, to one asking "whence is derived the custom of setting up May-poles, and dressing them with garlands; and what is the reason that the milk-maids dance before their customers' doors *with their pails dressed up with plate?*" it is answered: "It was a custom among the ancient Britons, before converted to Christianity, to erect these May-poles, adorned with flowers, in honour of the goddess Flora; and the dancing of the milk-maids may be only a corruption of that custom in complyance with the town."

> ## "*The Tears of Old May-Day.*
>
> "To her no more Augusta's wealthy pride
> Pours the full tribute from Potosi's mine;
> Nor fresh-blown garlands village-maids provide,
> A purer offering at her rustic shrine.
>
> No more the May-pole's verdant height around,
> To valour's games th' ambitious youths advance;
> No merry bells and tabor's sprightly sound
> Wake the loud carol and the sportive dance."

MORRIS-DANCERS.

THE Morris-dance, in which bells are gingled, or staves or swords clashed, was learned, says Dr. Johnson, by the Moors, and was probably a kind of Pyrrhic, or military dance.

"Morisco," says Blount, "(*Span.*) a Moor; also a dance, so called, wherein there were usually five men, and a boy dressed in a girl's habit, whom they called the Maid Marrion, or perhaps Morian, from the Italian Morione, a head-piece, because her head was wont to be gaily trimmed up. Common people call it a Morris-dance."

The Churchwardens' and Chamberlains' Books of Kingston-upon-Thames furnished Lysons with the following particulars illustrative of our subject, given in the Environs of London, i. 226 :—

		£	s.	d.
" 23 Hen. VII. To the menstorel upon May-day . . .		0	0	4
" For paynting of the *Mores* garments, and for serten gret leveres[1]		0	2	4
" For paynting of a bannar for Robin-hode		0	0	3
" For 2 M. and ½ pynnys		0	0	10
" For 4 plyts and ¼ of laun for the *Mores* garments		0	2	11
" For orseden [i. e. tinsel] for the same .		0	0	10
" For a goun for the lady . . .		0	0	8
" For bellys for the dawnsars . . .		0	0	12
24 Hen. VII. For Little John's cote . . .		0	8	0
1 Hen. VIII. For silver-paper for the *Mores* dawnsars		0	0	7
" For Kendall, for Robyn-hode's cotes .		0	1	3
" For 3 yerds of white for the frere's cote		0	3	0
" For 4 yerds of kendall for Mayd Marian's huke[2]		0	3	4
" For saten of sypers for the same hukee		0	0	6
" For 2 payre of glovys for Robyn-hode and Mayde Maryan		0	0	3

[1] The word *Livery* was formerly used to signify anything delivered: see the Northumberland Household Book, p. 60. If it ever bore such an acceptation at that time, one might be induced to suppose, from the following entries, that it here meant a badge, or something of that kind :—

	£	s.	d.
15 c. of leveres for Robin-hode . . .	0	5	0
For leveres, paper, and sateyn . . .	0	0	20
For pynnes and leveryes	0	6	5
For 13 c. of leverys	0	4	4
For 24 great lyverys	0	0	4

Probably these were a sort of cockades, given to the company from whom the money was collected.

[2] ["A kind of loose upper garment, sometimes furnished with a hood, and originally worn by men and soldiers, but in later times the term seems to have been applied exclusively to a sort of cloak worn by women,' Halliwell's Dictionary, p. 465.]

		£	s.	d.
1 Hen. VIII.	For 6 brode arouys	0	0	6
,,	To Mayde Marian, for her labour for two yeers	0	2	0
,,	To Fygge the taborer	0	6	0
,,	Rec^d for Robyn-hood's gaderyng 4 marks[1]			
5 Hen. VIII.	Rec^d for Robin-hood's gaderyng at Croydon	0	9	4
11 Hen. VIII.	Paid for three brode yerds of rosett for makyng the frer's cote	0	3	6
,,	Shoes for the *Mores daunsars*, the frere, and Mayde Maryan, at 7d. a peyre . . .	0	5	4
13 Hen. VIII.	Eight yerds of fustyan for the *Mores daunsars* coats	0	16	0
,,	A dosen of gold skynnes[2] for the *Morres* .	0	0	10
15 Hen. VIII.	Hire of hats for Robyn hode . . .	0	0	16
,,	Paid for the hat that was lost . . .	0	0	10
16 Hen. VIII.	Rec^d at the Church-ale and Robyn-hode, all things deducted	3	10	6
,,	Payd for 6 yerds ¼ of satyn for Robyn-hode's cotys	0	12	6
,,	For makyng the same	0	2	0
,,	For 3 ells of locram[3]	0	1	6
21 Hen. VIII.	For spunging and brushing Robyn-hode's cotys	0	0	2
28 Hen. VIII.	Five hats and 4 porses for the daunsars .	0	0	4½
,,	4 yerds of cloth for the fole's cote . .	0	2	0
,,	2 ells of worstede for Maide Maryan's kyrtle	0	6	8
,,	For 6 payre of double sollyd showne . .	0	4	6
,,	To the mynstrele	0	10	8
,,	To the fryer and the piper for to go to Croydon	0 · 0		8

" 29 Hen. VIII. Mem. lefte in the keping of the Wardens now beinge, a fryer's cote of russet, and a kyrtle of worsted weltyd with red cloth, a mowren's[4] cote of buckram, and 4 Morres daunsars cotes of white fustain spangelyd, and two gryne saten cotes, and a dysardd's[5] cote of cotton, and 6 payre of garters with bells." After this period, says Mr. Lysons, I find no entries relating to the above game.[6] It

[1] It appears that this, as well as other games, was made a parish concern.

[2] Probably gilt leather, the pliability of which was particularly accommodated to the motion of the dancers.

[3] A sort of coarse linen.

[4] Probably a Moor's coat; the word Morian is sometimes used to express a Moor. · Black buckram appears to have been much used for the dresses of the ancient mummers.

[5] Disard is an old word for a fool.

[6] In the Churchwardens' Accounts of Great Marlow, it appears that dresses for the Morris Dance "were lent out to the neighbouring parishes. They are accounted for so late as 1629." See Langley's Antiquities of Desborough, 4to. 1797, p. 142.

was so much in fashion in the reign of Henry VIII. that the king and his nobles would sometimes appear in disguise as Robin Hood and his men, dressed in Kendal, with hoods and hosen. See Holinshed's Chron. iii. 805.

In Coates's History of Reading, p. 130, Churchwardens' Accounts of St. Mary's parish, we have, in 1557,—

	£	s.	d.
Item, payed to the Mynstrels and the Hobby Horse uppon May Day	0	3	0
Item, payed to the Morrys Daunsers and the Mynstrelles, mete and drink at Whitsontide	0	3	4
Payed to them the Sonday after May Day . . .	0	0	20
Pd to the Painter for painting of their cotes	0	2	8
Pd to the Painter for 2 dz. of Lyveryes	0	0	20

In the rare tract of the time of Queen Elizabeth, entitled Plaine Percevall the Peace-maker of England, mention is made of a "stranger, which, seeing a quintessence (beside the Foole and the Maid Marian) of all the picked youth, strained out of a whole endship, footing the Morris about a May-pole, and he not hearing the minstrelsie for the fidling, the tune for the sound, nor the pipe for the noise of the tabor, bluntly demaunded if they were not all beside themselves, that they so lip'd and skip'd without an occasion."

Shakespeare makes mention of an English Whitson Morrice-dance, in the following speech of the Dauphin in Henry V. :—

> " No, with no more, than if we heard that England
> Were busied with a Whitson Morrice-dance."

"The English were famed," says Dr. Grey, "for these and such like diversions ; and even the old as well as young persons formerly followed them : a remarkable instance of which is given by Sir William Temple, (Miscellanea, Part 3, Essay of Health and Long Life,) who makes mention of a Morrice Dance in Herefordshire, from a noble person, who told him he had a pamphlet in his library, written by a very ingenious gentleman of that county, which gave an account how, in such a year of King James's reign, there went about the country a sett of Morrice-dancers, composed of ten men, who danced a Maid Marrian, and a tabor and pipe: and how these ten, one with another, made up twelve hundred years.

'Tis not so much, says he, that so many in one county should live to that age, as that they should be in vigour and humour to travel and dance." (Notes on Shakspeare, i. 382.)

The following description of a Morris-dance occurs in a very rare old poem, entitled Cobbe's Prophecies, his Signes and Tokens, his Madrigalls, Questions and Answers, 1614:—

> " It was my hap of late, by chance,
> To meet a country Morris-dance,
> When, cheefest of them all, the Foole
> Plaied with a ladle and a toole ;
> When every younker shak't his bels,
> Till sweating feete gave fohing smels :
> And fine Maide Marian with her smoile
> Shew'd how a rascall plaid the roile :
> But when the hobby-horse did wihy,
> Then all the wenches gave a tihy :
> But when they gan to shake their boxe,
> And not a goose could catch a foxe,
> The piper then put up his pipes,
> And all the woodcocks look't like snipes."

As is the following in Cotgrave's English Treasury of Wit and Language, 1655, p. 56 :—

> " How they become the Morris, with whose bells
> They ring all in to Whitson Ales, and sweat
> Through twenty scarfs and napkins, till the hobby horse
> Tire, and the Maid Marian, resolved to jelly,
> Be kept for spoon-meat."

[Compare, also, the following curious song printed in Wits Recreations, 1640 :—

> " With a noyse and a din,
> Comes the Maurice-dancer in,
> With a fine linnen shirt, but a buckram skin.
> Oh ! he treads out such a peale
> From his paire of legs of veale,
> The quarters are idols to him.
>
> Nor do those knaves inviron
> Their toes with so much iron,
> 'Twill ruine a smith to shooe him.
> I, and then he flings about,
> His sweat and his clout,
> The wiser think it two ells :
> While the yeomen find it meet
> That he jingle at his feet,
> The fore-horses' right eare jewels."]

We have an allusion to the Morris-dancer in the preface to Mythomistes, a tract of the time of Charles I. "Yet such helpes, as if nature have not beforehand in his byrth, given a Poet, all such forced art will come behind as lame to the businesse, and deficient as *the best taught countrey Morris-dauncer, with all his bells and napkins,* will ill deserve to be, *in an Inne of Courte at Christmas,* tearmed the thing they call *a fine reveller.*"

Stevenson, in the Twelve Months, 1661, p. 17, speaking of April, tells us: "The youth of the country make ready for the Morris-dance, and the merry milkmaid supplies them with ribbands her true love had given her." In Articles of Visitation and Inquiry for the Diocese of St. David, 1662, I find the following article: "Have no minstrels, no *Morris-dancers,* no dogs, hawks, or hounds, been suffered to be brought or come into your church, to the disturbance of the congregation?" Waldron, in his edition of the Sad Shepherd, 1783, p. 255, mentions seeing a company of Morrice-dancers from Abington, at Richmond, in Surrey, so late as the summer of 1783. They appeared to be making a kind of annual circuit. A few years ago, a May-game, or Morrice-dance, was performed by the following eight men in Herefordshire, whose ages, computed together, amounted to 800 years: J. Corley, aged 109; Thomas Buckley, 106; John Snow, 101; John Edey, 104; George Bailey, 106; Joseph Medbury, 100; John Medbury, 95; Joseph Pidgeon, 79.

Since these notes were collected, a Dissertation on the ancient English Morris Dance has appeared, from the pen of Mr. Douce, at the end of the second volume of his Illustrations of Shakespeare. Both English and foreign glossaries, he observes, uniformly ascribe the origin of this dance to the Moors: although the genuine Moorish or Morisco dance was, no doubt, very different from the European Morris. Strutt, in his Sports and Pastimes of the People of England, has cited a passage from the play of Variety, 1649, in which the Spanish Morisco is mentioned. And this, he adds, not only shows the legitimacy of the term Morris, but that the real and uncorrupted Moorish dance was to be found in Spain, where it still continues to delight both natives and foreigners, under the name of the *Fandango.* The Spanish Morrice was also danced at puppet-shows by a person habited like a Moor, with castagnets; and Junius has informed us that the Morris-dancers usually blackened their faces with soot, that they might the better pass for Moors.

Having noticed the corruption of the *Pyrrhica Saltatio* of the ancients, and the *uncorrupted Morris-dance*, as practised in France about the beginning of the thirteenth century, Douce says: " It has been supposed that the Morris-dance was first brought into England in the time of Edward the Third, when John of Gaunt returned from Spain (see Peck's Memoirs of Milton, p. 135), but it is much more probable that we had it from our Gallic neighbours, or even from the Flemings. Few, if any, vestiges of it can be traced beyond the time of Henry the Seventh, about which time, and particularly in that of Henry the Eighth, the churchwardens' accounts in several parishes afford materials that throw much light on the subject, and show that the Morris-dance made a very considerable figure in the parochial festivals. We find, also, that other festivals and ceremonies had their Morris; as, Holy Thursday; the Whitsun Ales; the Bride Ales, or Weddings; and a sort of play, or pageant, called the Lord of Misrule. Sheriffs, too, had their Morris-dance."

" The May-games of Robin Hood," it is observed, " appear to have been principally instituted for the encouragement of archery, and were generally accompanied by Morris-dancers, who, nevertheless, formed but a subordinate part of the ceremony. It is by no means clear that, at any time, Robin Hood and his companions were *constituent* characters in the Morris. In Laneham's Letter from Kenilworth, or Killingworth Castle, a Bride Ale is described, in which mention is made of ' a lively Moris dauns, according to *the auncient manner :* six dauncerz, Mawd-marion, and the fool.' "

MAID MARIAN, OR QUEEN OF THE MAY.

In Pasquill and Marforius, 1589, we read of " the May-game of Martinisme, verie defflie set out, with pompes, pagents, motions, maskes, scutchions, emblems, impreases, strange tricks and devises, betweene the ape and the owle ; the like was never yet seene in Paris Garden. Penry the Welchman is *the foregallant of the Morrice* with the treble belles, shot through the wit with a woodcock's bill. I would not for the fayrest horne-beast in all his countrey, that the Church of England were a cup of metheglin, and came in his way when he is overheated; every Bishopricke would procure but a draught, when the mazer is at his nose. Martin himselfe is the *Mayd-Marian*, trimlie drest uppe in a cast gowne, and a kercher of Dame Lawson's, his face handsomelie muffled with a diaper napkin to cover his beard, and a great nose-gay in his hande of the principalest flowers I could gather out of all hys works. Wiggenton daunces round about him in a cotten-coate, *to court him with a leatherne pudding and' a wooden ladle.* Paget *marshalleth the way* with a couple of great clubbes, one in his foote, another in his head, and he cries to the people, with a loude voice, ' Beware of the man whom God hath markt.' I cannot yet finde any so fitte to come lagging behind, with a budget on his necke *to gather the devotion of the lookers on,* as the stocke-keeper of the Bridewelhouse of Canterburie; he must *carry the purse to defray their charges,* and then hee may be sure to serve himselfe."

[Maid Marian is alluded to in the following very curious lines in a MS. of the fifteenth century:—

" At Ewle we wonten gambole, daunse, to carol, and to sing,
To have gud spiced sewe, and roste, and plum pie for a king;
At Easter Eve, pampuffes; Gangtide-Gates did olie masses bring;
At Paske begun oure Morris, and ere Pentecoste oure May,
Tho' Roben Hood, liell John, Frier Tuck, and Mariam deftly play,
And lord and ladie gang 'till kirk with lads and lasses gay;
Fra masse and een songe sa gud cheere and glee on every green,
As save oure wakes 'twixt Eames and Sibbes, like gam was never seene.
At Baptis-day, with ale and cakes, bout bonfires neighbours stood;
At Martlemas wa turn'd a crabbe, thilk told of Roben Hood,
Till after long time myrke, when blest were windowes, dores, and lightes,
And pailes were fild, and harthes were swept, gainst fairie elves and sprites:
Rock and Plow-Monday gams sal gang with saint feasts and kirk sightes."]

Tollett, in his Description of the Morris Dancers upon his Window, thus describes the celebrated Maid Marian, who, as Queen of May, has a golden crown on her head, and in her left hand a red pink, as emblem of Summer. Her vesture was once fashionable in the highest degree. Margaret, the eldest daughter of Henry VII., was married to James King of Scotland with the crown upon her head and her hair hanging down. Betwixt the crown and the hair was a very rich coif, hanging down behind the whole length of the body. This simple example sufficiently explains the dress of Marian's head. Her coif is purple, her surcoat blue, her cuffs white, the skirts of her robe yellow, the sleeves of a carnation colour, and her stomacher red, with a yellow lace in cross bars. In Shakespeare's play of Henry the Eighth, Anne Boleyn, at her coronation, is in her hair, or, as Holinshed says, her hair hanged down, but on her head she had a coif, with a circlet about it full of rich stones.[1]

In Greene's Quip for an upstart Courtier, 1620, f. 11, that effeminate-looking young man, we are told, used to act the part of Maid Marian, "to make the foole as faire, forsooth, as if he were to play Maid Marian in a May-game or a Morris-dance." In Shakerley Marmion's Antiquary, act iv., is the following passage : "A merry world the while, my boy and I, next Midsommer Ale, *I* may serve for a fool, and *he* for Maid Marrian." Shakespeare, Hen. IV., Part I., act iii. sc. 3, speaks of Maid Marian in her degraded state. It appears by one of the extracts already given from Lysons's Environs of London, that in the reign of Henry VIII., at Kingston-upon-Thames, the character was performed by a woman who received a shilling each year for her trouble. In Braithwaite's Strappado for the Divell, 1615, p. 63, is the following passage:—

——— " As for his bloud,
He says he can deriv't from Robin Hood
And his May-Marian, and I thinke he may,
For's mother plaid May-Marian t'other day."

Douce, however, considers the character of Marian as a dramatic fiction : "None of the materials," he observes, "that constitute the more authentic history of Robin Hood, prove the existence of such a character in the shape of his mistress. There is a pretty French pastoral drama of the eleventh or twelfth century, entitled *Le Jeu de Berger et de la Bergère,*

---

[1] In Coates's History of Reading, 1802, p. 220, in the Churchwardens' Accounts of St. Lawrence parish is the following entry : " 1531. It. for ffyve ells of canvas for a cote for Made Maryon, at iij^d. ob. the ell., xvij^d. ob."

in which the principal characters are *Robin* and *Marion*, a shepherd and shepherdess. Warton thought that our English Marian might be illustrated from this composition; but Ritson is unwilling to assent to this opinion, on the ground that the French Robin and Marion are not the 'Robin and Marian of Sherwood.' Yet Warton probably meant no more than that the name of Marian had been suggested from the above drama, which was a great favourite among the common people in France, and performed much about the season at which the May-games were celebrated in England. The great intercourse between the countries might have been the means of importing this name amidst an infinite variety of other matters; and there is indeed no other mode of accounting for the introduction of a name which never occurs in the page of English history. The story of Robin Hood was, at a very early period, of a dramatic cast; and it was perfectly natural that a principal character should be transferred from one drama to another. It might be thought, likewise, that the English Robin deserved his Marian as well as the other. The circumstance of the French Marian being acted by a boy contributes to support the above opinion; the part of the English character having been personated, though not always, in like manner."

After the Morris degenerated into a piece of coarse buffoonery, and Maid Marian was personated by a clown, this once elegant Queen of May obtained the name of Malkin. To this Beaumont and Fletcher allude in Monsieur Thomas :—

> " Put on the shape of order and humanity,
> Or you must marry *Malkyn*, the May lady."

Percy and Steevens agree in making Maid Marian the mistress of Robin Hood. It appears from the old play of the Downfall of Robert Earl of Huntingdon, 1601, that Maid Marian was originally a name assumed by Matilda, the daughter of Robert Lord Fitzwalter, while Robin Hood remained in a state of outlawry :

> " Next 'tis agreed (if thereto shee agree)
> That faire Matilda henceforth change her name ;
> And while it is the chance of Robin Hoode
> To live in Sherewodde a poore outlaw's life,
> She by Maid Marian's name be only call'd.
>
> *Mat.* I am contented ; reade on, little John :
> Henceforth let me be nam'd *Maide Marian*."

This lady was poisoned by King John at Dunmow Priory, after he had made several fruitless attempts on her chastity. Drayton has written her legend.

> [" In this our spacious isle I think there is not one,
> But he hath heard some talk of him [Hood] and Little John;
> Of Tuck, the merry Friar, which many a sermon made
> In praise of Robin Hood, his outlaws and their trade;
> Of Robin's mistress dear, his loved Marian,
> Was sovereign of the woods, chief lady of the game;
> Her clothes tuck'd to the knee, and dainty braided hair,
> With bow and quiver arm'd."
> *Drayton's Polyolbion*, Song 26.

So also Warner, in Albion's England,—

> " Tho' Robin Hood, liell John, Frier Tucke,
> And Marian deftly play;
> And lord and ladie gang till kirke
> With lads and lasses gay."]

Waldron, in his Description of the Isle of Man, (Works, p. 154,) tells us that the month of May is there every year ushered in with the following ceremony: " In almost all the great parishes, they choose from among the daughters of the most wealthy farmers a young maid for the *Queen of May*. She is drest in the gayest and best manner they can, and is attended by about twenty others, who are called maids of honour: she has also a young man who is her captain, and has under his command a good number of inferior officers. In opposition to her is the *Queen of Winter*, who is a man dressed in woman's clothes, with woollen hoods, furr tippets, and loaded with the warmest and heaviest habits one upon another: in the same manner are those who represent her attendants drest, nor is she without a captain and troop for her defence. Both being equipt as proper emblems of the beauty of the Spring, and the deformity of the Winter, they set forth from their respective quarters; the one preceded by violins and flutes, the other with the rough musick of the tongs and cleavers. Both companies march till they meet on a common, and then their trains engage in a mock battle. If the Queen of Winter's forces get the better, so far as to take the Queen of May prisoner, she is ransomed for as much as pays the expences of the day. After this ceremony, Winter and her company retire, and divert themselves in a barn, and

17

the others remain on the green, where, having danced a considerable time, they conclude the evening with a feast: the Queen at one table with her maids, the Captain with his troop at another. There are seldom less than fifty or sixty persons at each board, but not more than three knives."

Douce says, "It appears that the Lady of the May was sometimes carried in procession on men's shoulders; for Stephen Batman, speaking of the Pope and his ceremonies, states that he is carried on the backs of four deacons, 'after the manner of carying Whytepot Queenes in Western May Games.'" He adds, "There can be no doubt that the Queen of May is the legitimate representative of the Goddess Flora in the Roman Festival."

In the Gentleman's Magazine for Oct. 1793, p. 188, there is a curious anecdote of Dr. Geddes, the well-known translator of the Bible, who, it should seem, was fond of innocent festivities. He was seen in the summer of that year, "*mounted on the poles behind the Queen of the May* at Marsden Fair, in Oxfordshire."

[A very curious tract appeared in 1609, entitled, 'Old Meg of Herefordshire for a Maid Marian, and Hereford Towne for a Morris Dance, or twelve Morris dancers in Herefordshire of twelve hundred years old.' It gives us, however, very few particulars respecting the manner of conducting the morris, the humour of the author being chiefly occupied with the extreme age of the performers. "And howe doe you like this Morris dance of Herefordshire? Are they not brave olde youths? Have they not the right footing? the true tread? comely lifting up of one legge, and active bestowing of the other? Kemp's morris to Norwich was no more to this than a galliard on the common stage at the end of an old dead comedie is to a caranto daunced on the ropes."]

ROBIN HOOD.

Bishop Latimer, in his sixth sermon before King Edward VI., mentions Robin Hood's Day, kept by country people in memory of him. "I came once myself," says he, "to a place, riding a journey homeward from London, and sent word overnight into the town that I would preach there in the morning, because it was a holy-day, and I took my horse and my company and went thither (I thought I should have found a great company in the church); when I came there, the church door was fast locked. I tarried there half an hour and more; at last the key was found, and one of the parish comes to me and says : 'This is a busy day with us, we cannot heare you ; this is Robin Hoode's daye, the parish is gone abroad to gather for Robin Hoode.' I thought my rochet should have been regarded, though I were not : but it would not serve, but was fayne to give place to Robin Hoode's men."[1]

We read, in Skene's Regiam Majestatem, " Gif anie provest, baillie, counsell, or communitie, chuse *Robert Hude*, litell John, Abbat of Unreason, *Queens of Maii*, the chusers sall tyne their friedome for five zeares ; and sall bee punished at the King's will; and the accepter of sick ane office salbe banished furth of the realme." And under " pecuniall crimes," —" all persons, quha a landwort, or within burgh, chuses *Robert Hude*, sall pay ten pounds, and sall be warded induring the King's pleasure."[2]

Douce thinks " the introduction of Robin Hood into the celebration of May, probably suggested the addition of a *King* or *Lord of May*." The Summer *King* and *Queen*, or *Lord* and *Lady of the May*, however, are characters of very high antiquity. In the Synod at Worcester, A.D. 1240, can. 38, a strict command was given, " Ne intersint ludis inhonestis nec

---

[1] In Coates's History of Reading, p. 214, in the Churchwardens' Accounts of St. Lawrence Parish, 1499, is the following article : " It. rec. of the *gaderyng* of Robyn-hod, xixs." In the Churchwardens' Accounts of St. Helen's, Abingdon, 1566, we find eighteen pence charged for setting up Robin Hood's bower. See Nichols's Illustrations of Ancient Manners and Expences, p. 143.

[2] Ihre, in his Suio-Gothic Glossary, makes the following mention of the King or Lord of May upon the Continent :—" Maigrefwe dicebatur, qui mense Maijo serto floreo redimitus solenni pompa per plateas et vicos circumducebatur. Commemorant Historici, Gustavum I. Suionum Regem anno 1526, sub nundinis Ericianis vel d. 18. Maii ejusmodi *Comitem Majum* creasse Johannem Magnum, Archiep. Upsaliensem. Et quum moris esset, ut Comes hic imaginarius satellitium, quod eum stipaverat, convivio exciperet, fecit id Johannes non sine ingenti impensa, ut ipse in Historia Metropolitana conqueritur. Conf. Westenhielms Hist. Gust. I. ad annum, necnon Tegel in Historia hujus Reg. Part. 1. In Anglia quoque ejusmodi Reges et Reginæ Majales floribus ornati a juventute olim creabantur, quo facto circa perticam eminentiorem, nostris Maistang dictam, choreas ducebant, et varios alios ludos exercebant." Tom. ii. p. 118, sub *v*.

sustineant *ludos fieri de rege et regina,* nec arietes levari, nec palestras publicas."[1]

Lysons, in his extracts from the Churchwardens' and Chamberlains' Accounts at Kingston-upon Thames, affords us some curious particulars of a sport called the " Kyngham," or King-game. "Be yt in mynd, that the 19 yere of King Harry the 7, at the geveng out of the Kynggam by Harry Bower and Harry Nycol, cherchewardens, amounted clerely to £4. 2*s.* 6*d.* of that same game.

	£	*s.*	*d.*
" Mem. That the 27 day of Joun, aº. 21 Kyng H. 7, that we, Adam Bakhous and Harry Nycol, hath made account for the Kenggam, that same tym don Wylm Kempe, *Kenge,* and Joan Whytebrede, *quen,* ånd all costs deducted	4	5	0
23 Hen. 7. Paid for whet and malt and vele and motton and pygges and ger and coks for the Kyngam . .	0	33	0
To the taberare	0	6	8
To the leutare	0	2	0
1 Hen. 8. Paid out of the Churche-box at Walton Kyngham	0	3	6
———— Paid to Robert Neyle for goyng to Wyndesore for maister doctor's horse agaynes the Kyngham day	0	4	0
———— For bakyng the Kyngham brede	0	0	6
———— To a laborer for bering home of the geere after the Kyngham was don	0	1	0"

The contributions to the celebration of the same game, Lysons observes, in the neighbouring parishes, show that the Kyngham was not confined to Kingston. In another quotation from the same accounts, 24 Hen. VII., the " cost of the *Kyngham* and *Robyn-hode*" appears in one entry, viz.

	£	*s.*	*d.*
" A kylderkin of 3 halfpennye bere and a kilderkin of singgyl bere	0	2	4
9 bushels of whete	0	6	3
2 bushels and ½ of rye	0	1	8
3 shepe	0	5	0
A lamb	0	1	4
2 calvys	0	5	4
6 pygges	0	2	0
3 bushell of colys	0	0	3
The coks for their labour	0	1	11½"

[1] [This passage is quoted by Kennett, in his Glossary, p. 15 in his explanation of the quintain.]

The clear profits, 15 Henry VIII. (the last time Lysons found it mentioned), amounted to £9 10s. 6d., a very considerable sum for that period.

In a comedy by Beaumont and Fletcher, entitled the Knight of the burning Pestle, 1613, Rafe, one of the characters, appears as Lord of the May:

> " And, by the common-councell of my fellows in the Strand,
>   With gilded staff, and crossed skarfe, the May-Lord here I stand."

He adds:

> " The Morrice rings while Hobby Horse doth foot it featously;"

and, addressing the group of citizens assembled around him, "from the top of Conduit-head," he says:

> " And lift aloft your velvet heads, and, slipping of your gowne,
>   With bells on legs, and napkins cleane unto your shoulders tide,
>   With scarfs and garters as you please, and hey for our town cry'd:
>   March out and shew your willing minds by twenty and by twenty,
>   To Hogsdon or to Newington, where ale and cakes are plenty.
>   And let it nere be said for shame, that we, the youths of London,
>   Lay thrumming of our caps at home, and left our custome undone.
>   Up then, I say, both young and old, both man and maid, a Maying,
>   With drums and guns that bounce aloude, and merry taber playing."

In Sir David Dalrymple's extracts from the Book of the Universal Kirk, in the year 1576, Robin Hood is styled *King of May*.

[The following curious account is extracted from Stow's Survay of London, 1603, p. 98: " In the moneth of May, namely on May-day in the morning, every man, except impediment, would walke into the sweete meadowes and greene woods, there to rejoyce their spirites with the beauty and savour of sweete flowers, and with the harmony of birds, praysing God in their kind, and for example hereof, Edward Hall hath noted that K. Henry the Eight, as in the 3. of his raigne and divers other yeares, so namely in the seaventh of his raigne, on May-day in the morning, with Queene Katheren his wife, accompanied with many lords and ladies, rode a Maying from Greenwitch to the high ground of Shooters Hill, whereas they passed by the way, they espied a companie of tall yeomen cloathed all in greene, with greene whoodes, and with bowes and arrowes to the number of two hundred. One, being their chieftaine, was called Robin Hoode, who required the king and his companie to stay and see his men shoote, whereunto the king graunting, Robin Hoode whistled, and all the 200 archers shot off, loosing all at once, and when he whistled againe, they likewise shot againe, their arrowes whistled by craft of the head, so that the noyse was straunge and loude, which greatly delighted the king, queene, and their companie. Moreover, this Robin Hoode desired the king and queene, with their retinue, to enter the greene wood, where, in harbours made of boughes and decked with flowers, they were set and served plentifully with venison and wine by Robin Hoode and his meynie, to their great contentment, and had other pageants and pastimes." This description has been already slightly alluded to.]

FRIAR TUCK.

Tollett describes this character upon his window, as in the full clerical tonsure, with a chaplet of white and red beads in his right hand : and, expressive of his professed humility, his eyes are cast upon the ground. His corded girdle and his russet habit denote him to be of the Franciscan Order, or one of the Grey Friars. His stockings are red; his red girdle is ornamented with a golden twist, and with a golden tassel. At his girdle hangs a wallet for the reception of provision, the only revenue of the mendicant orders of religious, who were named Walleteers, or Budget-bearers. Steevens supposes this Morris Friar designed for Friar Tuck, chaplain to Robin Hood, as King of May. He is mentioned by Drayton, in lines already quoted at p. 257.

He is known to have formed one of the characters in the May-games during the reign of Henry the Eighth, and had been probably introduced into them at a much earlier period. From the occurrence of this name on other occasions, there is good reason for supposing that it was a sort of generic appellation for any friar, and that it originated from the dress of the order, which was *tucked* or folded at the waist by means of a cord or girdle. Thus Chaucer, in his Prologue to the Canterbury Tales, says of the Reve :

" *Tucked* he was, as is a frere aboute :"

and he describes one of the friars in the Sompnour's Tale :

" With scrippe and tipped staff, *y-tucked* hie."

This Friar maintained his situation in the Morris under the

reign of Elizabeth, being thus mentioned in Warner's Albion's England :

Tho' Robin Hood, litell John, *frier Tucke*, and Marian, deftly play:

but is not heard of afterwards. In Ben Jonson's Masque of Gipsies, the clown takes notice of his omission in the dance : " There is no Maid Marian nor Friar amongst them, which is a surer mark."

The Friar's coat, as appears from some of the extracts of Churchwardens' and Chamberlains' Accounts of Kingston, already quoted, was generally of russet. In an ancient drama, called the Play of Robin Hood, very proper to be played in May-games, a friar, whose name is Tuck, is one of the principal characters. He comes to the forest in search of Robin Hood, with an intention to fight him, but consents to become chaplain to his lady.

THE FOOL.

Tollett, describing the Morris-dancers in his window, calls this the counterfeit Fool, that was kept in the royal palace, and in all great houses, to make sport for the family. He appears with all the badges of his office; *the bauble in his hand, and a coxcomb hood, with asses' ears, on his head.* The top of the hood rises into the form of a cock's neck and head, with a bell at the latter: and Minshew's Dictionary, 1627, under the word Cock's-comb, observes, that " natural idiots and fools have [accustomed] and still do accustome themselves to weare in their cappes cocke's feathers, or a hat with the necke and head of a cocke on the top, and a bell thereon." His hood is blue, guarded or edged with yellow at its scalloped bottom ; his doublet is red, striped across, or rayed, with a deeper red, and edged with yellow ; his girdle yellow ; his left-side hose yellow, with a red shoe ; and his right-side hose blue, soled with red leather.[1]

In the Churchwardens' Accounts of the parish of St. Helen's,

---

[1] There is in Olaus Magnus, 1555, p. 524, a delineation of a Fool, or Jester, with several bells upon his habit, with a bauble in his hand ; and he has on his head a hood with asses' ears, a feather, and the resemblance of the comb of a cock. It seems, from the Prologue to the play of King Henry the Eighth, that Shakespeare's Fools should be dressed " in *a long motley coat guarded with yellow.*"

in Abingdon, Berkshire, from Phil. & Mar., to 34 Eliz., the *Morrice* bells are mentioned: 1560,—" For two dossin of Morres bells." As these appear to have been purchased by the community, we may suppose the diversion of the Morris-dance was constantly practised at their public festivals. " Bells for the dancers" have been already noticed in the Churchwardens' Accounts of Kingston-upon-Thames: and they are mentioned in those of St. Mary-at-Hill, in the city of London.

Morrice-dancing, *with bells on the legs,* was common in Oxfordshire, and the adjacent counties, on May-day, Holy Thursday, and Whitsun Ales, attended by the Fool, or, as he was generally called, the Squire, and also a lord and lady; the latter, most probably, the Maid Marian mentioned in Mr. Tollett's note: nor was the Hobby-horse forgot. The custom is by no means obsolete.

In the Knave of Hearts we read,—

> " My *sleeves* are like some Morris-dansing fello,
> My stockings, *ideot-like, red, greene, yellow.*"

Steevens observes : " When fools were kept for diversion in great families, they were distinguished by a calf-skin coat, which had the buttons down the back; and this they wore that they might be known for fools, and escape the resentment of those whom they provoked with their waggeries. The custom is still preserved in Ireland; and the Fool, in any of the legends which the mummers act at Christmas, always appears in a calf's or cow's skin."

" The properties belonging to this strange personage," says Strutt, " in the early times, are little known at present; they were such, however, as recommended him to the notice of his superiors, and rendered his presence a sort of requisite in the houses of the opulent. According to the illuminators of the thirteenth century, he bears the squalid appearance of a wretched idiot, wrapped in a blanket which scarcely covers his nakedness, holding in one hand a stick, with an inflated bladder attached to it by a cord, which answered the purpose of a bauble. If we view him in his more improved state, where his clothing is something better, yet his tricks[1] are so

---

[1] " In one instance he is biting the tail of a dog, and seems to place his fingers upon his body, as if he were stopping the holes of a flute, and

exceedingly barbarous and vulgar, that they would disgrace
the most despicable Jack-pudding that ever exhibited at Bartholomew Fair : and even when he was more perfectly equip-
ped in his party-coloured coat and hood, and completely de-
corated with bells,[1] his improvements are of such a nature
as seem to add but little to his respectability, much less qua-
lify him as a companion for kings and noblemen. In the six-
teenth and seventeenth centuries the fool, or more properly
the jester, was a man of some ability ; and, if his character has
been strictly drawn by Shakespeare and other dramatic
writers, the entertainment he afforded consisted in witty
retorts and sarcastical reflections ; and his licence seems,
upon such occasions, to have been very extensive. Sometimes,
however, these gentlemen overpassed the appointed limits,
and they were, therefore, corrected or discharged. The latter
misfortune happened to Archibald Armstrong, jester to King
Charles the First. The wag happened to pass a severe jest
upon Laud, Archbishop of Canterbury, which so highly
offended the supercilious prelate, that he procured an order
from the King in council for his discharge."[2]

---

probably moved them as the animal altered its cry. The other is riding
on a stick with a bell, having a blown bladder attached to it."

[1] " This figure," referred to by Strutt, " has a stick surmounted with a
bladder, if I mistake not, which is in lieu of a bauble, which we frequently
see representing a fool's head, with hood and bells, and a cock's comb
upon the hood, very handsomely carved." William Summers, jester to
Henry the Eighth, was habited "in a motley jerkin, with motley hosen."
—*History of Jack of Newbury.*

[2] The order for Archy's discharge was as follows : " It is, this day,
(March 11, 1637,) ordered by his Majesty, with the advice of the board,
that Archibald Armstrong, the King's Fool, for certain scandalous words,
of a high nature, spoken by him against the Lord Archbishop of Canterbury, his Grace, and proved to be uttered by him by two witnesses, shall
have his coat pulled over his head, and be discharged the king's service,
and banished the court; for which the Lord Chamberlain of the King's
household is prayed and required to give order to be executed." And im-
mediately the same was put in execution.—*Rushworth's Collections,* part 2,
vol. i. p. 471. The same authority, p. 470, says, " It 'so happened that,
on the 11th of the said March, that Archibald, the King's Fool, said to his
Grace the Archbishop of Canterbury, as he was going to the council-table,
' Whea's feule now ? Doth not your Grace hear the news from Striveling
about the Liturgy ?' with other words of reflection. This was presently
complained of to the council, which produced the ensuing order."

SCARLET, STOKESLEY, AND LITTLE JOHN.

These appear to have been Robin Hood's companions, from the following old ballad :—

> " I have heard talk of Robin Hood,
> Derry, Derry, Derry down,
> And of brave *Little John*,
> Of Friar Tuck and *Will Scarlet*,
> *Stokesley* and Maid Marrian,
> Hey down," &c.

Among the extracts given by Lysons, from the Church-wardens' and Chamberlains' Accounts of Kingston-upon-Thames, an entry has been already quoted " for Little John's cote." Douce says, Little John " is first mentioned, together with Robin Hood, by Fordun, the Scottish historian, who wrote in the fourteenth century (Scotichron. ii. 104), and who speaks of the celebration of the story of these persons in the theatrical performances of his time, and of the minstrels' songs relating to them, which he says the common people preferred to all other romances."

TOM THE PIPER, WITH TABOUR AND PIPE.

Among the extracts already quoted in a note from Lysons's Environs of London, there is one entry which shows that the Piper was sent (probably to make collections) round the country. Tollett, in the description of his window, says, to prove No. 9 to be Tom the Piper, Steevens has very happily quoted these lines from Drayton's third Eclogue :—

> " Myself above Tom Piper to advance,
> Who so bestirs him in the Morris-dance,
> For penny wage."

His tabour, tabour-stick, and pipe attest his profession; the feather in his cap, his sword, and silver-tinctured shield[1] may denote him to be a squire-minstrel, or a minstrel of the superior order. Chaucer, 1721, p. 181, says: " Minstrels

---

[1] Douce says: " What Mr. Tollett has termed his *silver shield* seems a mistake for the lower part, or flap, of his stomacher."—*Illustr. of Shaksp* ii. 463.

used a red hat." Tom Piper's bonnet is red, faced or turned up with yellow, his doublet blue, the sleeves blue, turned up with yellow, something like red muffetees at his wrists ; over his doublet is a red garment, like a short cloak with arm-holes, and with a yellow cape ; his hose red, and garnished across and perpendicularly on the thighs with a narrow yellow lace. His shoes are brown.

THE HOBBY-HORSE.

Tollett, in his description of the Morris-dancers in his window, is induced to think the famous Hobby-horse to be the King of the May, though he now appears as a juggler and a buffoon, from the crimson foot-cloth,[1] fretted with gold, the golden bit, the purple bridle, with a golden tassel, and studded with gold, the man's purple mantle with a golden border, which is latticed with purple, his golden crown, purple cap, with a red feather and with a golden knop. "Our Hobby," he adds, "is a spirited horse of pasteboard, in which the master dances and displays tricks of legerdemain, such as the threading of the needle, the mimicking of the whigh-hie, and the daggers in the nose, &c., as Ben Jonson acquaints us, and thereby explains the swords in the man's cheeks. What is stuck in the horse's mouth I apprehend to be a ladle, ornamented with a ribbon. Its use was to receive the spectators' pecuniary donations. The colour of the Hobby-horse is reddish-white, like the beautiful blossom of the peach-tree. The man's coat, or doublet, is the only one upon the window that has buttons upon it ; and the right side of it is yellow, and the left red."

In the old play of the Vow-Breaker, or the Fayre Maid of Clifton, 1636, by William Sampson, is the following dialogue between Miles, the Miller of Ruddington, and Ball, which throws great light upon this now obsolete character :—

---

[1] The foot-cloth, however, was used by the fool. In Braithwaite's Strappado for the Divell, we read:—

> "Erect our aged fortunes, make them shine,
> Not like *Foole in's foot-cloath*, but like Time
> Adorn'd with true experiments," &c.

"*Ball.* But who shall play the Hobby-horse? Master Major?

"*Miles.* I hope I looke as like a Hobby-horse as Master Major. I have not liv'd to these yeares, but a man woo'd thinke I should be old enough and wise enough to play the Hobby-horse as well as ever a Major on 'em all. Let the Major play the Hobby-horse among his brethren, an he will; I hope our towne ladds cannot want a Hobby-horse. Have I practic'd my reines, my carree'res, my pranckers, my ambles, my false trotts, my smooth ambles, and Canterbury paces, and shall Master Major put me besides the Hobby-horse? Have I borrowed the fore horse-bells, his plumes, and braveries, nay, had his mane new shorne and frizl'd, and shall the Major put me besides the Hobby-horse? Let him hobby-horse at home, and he will. Am I not going to buy ribbons and toyes of sweet Ursula for the *Marian,* and shall I not play the Hobby-horse?

"*Ball.* What shall Joshua doe?

"*Miles.* Not know of it, by any meanes; hee'l keepe more stir with the Hobby-horse then he did with the Pipers at Tedbury Bull-running: provide thou for the *Dragon,* and leave me for a Hobby-horse.

"*Ball.* Feare not, I'le be a fiery Dragon." And afterwards, when Boote askes him: "Miles, the Miller of Ruddington, gentleman and souldier, what make you here?"

"*Miles.* Alas, sir, to borrow a few ribbandes, bracelets, eare-rings, wyer-tyers, and silke girdles and hand-kerchers for a Morice, and a show before the Queene.

"*Boote.* Miles, you came to steale my neece.

"*Miles.* Oh Lord! Sir, I came to furnish the Hobby-horse.

"*Boote.* Get into your Hobby-horse gallop, and be gon then, or I'le Moris-dance you—Mistris, waite you on me. [*Exit.*

"*Ursula.* Farewell, good Hobby-horse.—*Weehee.*" [*Exit.*

Douce informs us, that the earliest vestige now remaining of the Hobby-horse is in the painted window at Betley, already described. The allusions to the omission of the Hobby-horse are frequent in the old plays; and the line,

For O, for O, the Hobby-horse is forgot,'

is termed by Hamlet an *epitaph,* which Theobald supposed, with great probability, to have been satirical.

[Compare also Ben Jonson, —

> [" But see, the Hobby-horse is forgot.
> Fool, it must be your lot
> To supply his want with faces,
> And some other buffon graces."]

A scene in Beaumont and Fletcher's Women Pleased, act iv., best shows the sentiments of the Puritans on this occasion.

[The following lines occur in a poem on London, in MS. Harl. 3910 :—

> " In Fleet strete then I heard a shoote :
> I putt off my hatt, and I made no staye,
> And when I came unto the rowte,
> Good Lord ! I heard a taber playe,

> For so, God save mee ! a Morrys-daunce :
> Oh ! ther was sport alone for mee,
> To see the *Hobby-horse* how he did praunce
> Among the gingling company.

> I proffer'd them money for their coats,
> But my conscience had remorse,
> For my father had no oates,
> And I must have had the Hobbie-horse."]

" Whoever," says Douce, " happens to recollect the manner in which Bayes's troops, in the Rehearsal, are exhibited on the stage, will have a tolerably correct notion of a Morris Hobby-horse. Additional remains of the Pyrrhic, or sword-dance, are preserved in the daggers stuck in the man's cheeks, which constituted one of the hocus-pocus or legerdemain tricks practised by this character, among which were the threading of a needle, and the transferring of an egg from one hand to the other, called by Ben Jonson, in his Every Man out of his Humour, *the travels of the egg*. To the horse's mouth was suspended a ladle, for the purpose of gathering money from the spectators. In later times the fool appears to have performed this office, as may be collected from Nashe's play of Summer's last Will and Testament, where this stage-direction occurs : 'Ver goes in and fetcheth out the Hobby-horse and the Morrice-daunce, who daunce about.' Ver then says: 'About, about, lively, put your horse to it, reyne him harder, jerke him with your wand, sit fast, sit fast, man: *Foole, hold up your ladle there.*' Will Summers is made to say, 'You friend with the Hobby-horse, goe not too fast, for fear of wearing out my lord's tyle-stones with your hob-nayles.' Afterwards there enter three clowns and three maids, who dance the Morris, and at the same time sing the following song :—

> ' Trip and goe, heave and hoe,
> Up and downe, to and fro,
> From the towne to the grove
> Two and two, let us rove,
> A Maying, a playing ;
> Love hath no gainsaying :
> So merrily trip and goe.' "

Lord Orford, in his Catalogue of English Engravers, under the article of Peter Stent, has described two paintings at Lord Fitzwilliam's, on Richmond Green, which came out of the old neighbouring palace. They were executed by Vincken-boom, about the end of the reign of James I., and exhibit views of the above palace : in one of these pictures a Morris-dance is introduced, consisting of seven figures, viz. " a fool, a Hobby-horse, a piper, a Maid Marian, and three other dancers, the rest of the figures being spectators." Of these, the first four and one of the dancers, Douce has reduced in a plate from a tracing made by the late Captain Grose. The fool has an inflated bladder, or eel-skin, with a ladle at the end of it, and with this he is collecting money. The piper is pretty much in his original state ; but the Hobby-horse wants the legerdemain apparatus, and Maid Marian is not remarkable for the elegance of her person.

A short time before the revolution in France, the May-games and Morris-dance were celebrated in many parts of that country, accompanied by a fool and a *Hobby-horse.* The latter was termed *un chevalet ;* and, if the authority of Minshew be not questionable, the Spaniards had the same character under the name of *tarasca.*[1]

[1] [A great deal of the above is literally transcribed from Douce's Illus-trations of Shakespeare.]

Lightning Source UK Ltd.
Milton Keynes UK
UKOW051920020912

198361UK00001B/137/P